A PRACTICAL GUIDE TO
TEACHER
WELLBEING

Sara Miller McCune founded SAGE Publishing in 1965 to support the dissemination of usable knowledge and educate a global community. SAGE publishes more than 1000 journals and over 800 new books each year, spanning a wide range of subject areas. Our growing selection of library products includes archives, data, case studies and video. SAGE remains majority owned by our founder and after her lifetime will become owned by a charitable trust that secures the company's continued independence.

Los Angeles | London | New Delhi | Singapore | Washington DC | Melbourne

ELIZABETH HOLMES

A PRACTICAL GUIDE TO
TEACHER
WELLBEING

Learning Matters
An imprint of SAGE Publications Ltd
1 Oliver's Yard
55 City Road
London EC1Y 1SP

SAGE Publications Inc.
2455 Teller Road
Thousand Oaks, California 91320

SAGE Publications India Pvt Ltd
B 1/I 1 Mohan Cooperative Industrial Area
Mathura Road
New Delhi 110 044

SAGE Publications Asia-Pacific Pte Ltd
3 Church Street
#10-04 Samsung Hub
Singapore 049483

© 2019 Elizabeth Holmes

First published 2019

Editor: Amy Thornton
Senior project editor: Chris Marke
Project management: Swales & Willis Ltd, Exeter, Devon
Marketing manager: Dilhara Attygalle
Cover design: Wendy Scott
Typeset by: C&M Digitals (P) Ltd, Chennai, India
Printed in the UK

Library of Congress Control Number: 2018957327

British Library Cataloguing in Publication Data

A catalogue record for this book is available from the British Library

ISBN 978-1-5264-4586-5
ISBN 978-1-5264-4587-2 (pbk)

At SAGE we take sustainability seriously. Most of our products are printed in the UK using responsibly sourced papers and boards. When we print overseas we ensure sustainable papers are used as measured by the PREPS grading system. We undertake an annual audit to monitor our sustainability.

For Michael – whose sheer joy of life and abundant love contributes immeasurably to my own wellbeing.

CONTENTS

THE AUTHOR

ELIZABETH HOLMES is a teacher, writer, lifelong learner, and mother with wide-ranging and varied experience in the world of education. She has written extensively on teacher wellbeing for a range of national and international publications and websites, and has worked with teachers all over the UK to help develop a greater understanding of wellbeing in education. Elizabeth currently teaches on initial teacher education courses at the University of Chichester. You can find out more about Elizabeth's work at elizabethholmes.info.

ACKNOWLEDGEMENTS

My gratitude, first and foremost, goes to the many teachers and trainees who have so honestly shared their thoughts and feelings about teacher wellbeing, and helped to shape this little text. In addition, I am grateful to the many hundreds if not thousands of teachers who have been a part of the conversation about teacher wellbeing over the last few decades, through the books and articles I have written, and professional development sessions I have led. Thank you.

Gratitude must also be extended to all the professionals in education working to improve teacher wellbeing on a daily basis – all the senior leaders, teachers and other school staff, the teacher unions' staff, the Education Support Partnership staff and everyone else who puts teacher wellbeing at the heart of what they do. Thank you.

Grateful thanks also to Dr Larry Culliford, who read chapters and offered incredibly insightful suggestions for improvements (at short notice I should add!). Larry's website is well worth a browse: **www.ldc52.co.uk**.

Dr Pooky Knightsmith was a brilliant conversation partner on the phone. Thank you Pooky! I recommend a peruse of Pooky's website too: **www.inourhands.com**.

Richard Docwra, a co-director and the powerful driving force of Life Squared, offered inspiration and clarity on all things wellbeing. His work for Life Squared is incredibly important for everyone. **www.lifesquared.org**.

Dr Miles Richardson was a great help in teaching me about the role of nature in our wellbeing. His blog, *Finding Nature*, is a must for all with an interest in wellbeing: **https://findingnature.org.uk**.

Dr Tim O'Brien, who reassured me I was on the right track with this book. Thank you.

Many teachers and other education professionals in my personal learning network in real life and on Twitter – what an amazing bunch you are! It's always a pleasure interacting with, and learning from, you. Thank you.

My agent, Charlotte Howard, who has supported my work for two decades now. I am immensely grateful. My fellow authors at the Fox and Howard Literary Agency, too, who never cease to inspire!

Amy Thornton at SAGE, whose vision, support, encouragement (and patience!) for this book is deeply appreciated. Thank you.

Finally, last but by no means least, my family, whose support for my own wellbeing knows no bounds. With a special mention for my parents, who are also the best entertainers of small people too! My gratitude and love.

INTRODUCTION

It is widely accepted that teaching is a stressful job. Workload, accountability, pupil behaviour, some of which is linked to the mental health struggles that so many children and young people have now, and a workforce that seems constantly to be operating at beyond full capacity, all contribute to the pressures felt in the profession, regardless of experience, or the age and stage taught.

Excessive stress in our professional lives is a crushing issue. Careers have ended because of it. Physical and mental health has crumbled. And it is not too much of a stretch to say that the teaching standards of those weighed down by it may be affected (see, for example, Dr Chris Dewberry and Professor Rob B. Briner's report published by Worklife Support in May 2007: Staff wellbeing is key to school success: a research study into the links between staff wellbeing and school performance). Excessive stress sucks the joy from life and renders us incapable of feeling in control of the tasks facing us. Life is no longer manageable, and at times we don't see any of that coming.

When I first started writing about teacher wellbeing in the mid-1990s, my main focus was on trainees and newly qualified teachers, but from the communications I received, many experienced teachers were undoubtedly struggling with workload at a time when relatively little was written about the whole concept of wellbeing in mainstream circles. The profession had undergone rapid change and was still coming to terms with the introduction of the Office for Standards in Education (OFSTED) earlier that decade. Inspections were lengthy and relied on extensive paperwork preparation ahead of the inspectors calling, while it was not unusual for individual teachers to be observed repeatedly in the course of a week-long inspection. Combine this with a seemingly rapid increase in workload and it is not surprising that wellbeing suffered.

In time, policymakers, employers, governors, initial teacher education courses, teacher unions, professional associations and others began to acknowledge that teacher wellbeing needed to be addressed. In 1999 Teacherline (which went on to become the Teacher Support Line) was established by the Teacher Support Network (formerly the Teacher Benevolent Fund, and now the Education Support Partnership). In 2017 alone, the Education Support Partnership dealt with 8793 cases.

Recently, the Education Support Partnership revealed that there has been a 35% increase in calls from teachers over the 12 months leading up to April 2018. The rise in calls from headteachers and deputy headteachers was 24%. Workplace stress, followed by work performance issues were the two most common reasons for education staff to call the helpline. There has also been an increase in calls about conflict at work and bullying or harassment.

Despite this evident downward trajectory in teacher wellbeing, it is extremely heartening to read about staff wellbeing teams and wellbeing champions in schools. While these ideas alone will never suffice, there are so many strategies that can help to contribute towards gently raising the levels of wellbeing felt by school staff members. But we must not overlook the fact that real transformation in our experience of wellbeing in our schools will come from structural shifts *as well as* highly personalised individual shifts. Ultimately the goal is for teachers to have a strong sense of what wellbeing means for us all, as individuals, *rather than* to build resilience in order to tolerate increasing levels of negative stress in a dysfunctional system.

When we experience a sense of wellbeing, we feel good and we function well. With a healthy dose of positive stress, we can excel at our work in the knowledge that our lives are balanced and fruitful. But this is not the experience of too many of our staff in schools today, and this must change.

As the author of this text (albeit with the help of a great many teachers, trainees and other experts in their fields) I am painfully aware that no book can suit all readers. Similarly, no book on teacher wellbeing can address each and every aspect of the lived experience of teaching that it needs to. For this reason, this is not a book about transforming organisations, ideologies and systems within schools in order to promote wellbeing. Neither does it seek to offer strategies for reforming planning, marking and assessment (although this is touched upon in Chapter 6). There are other (far lengthier) books which tackle this. This book is about developing a *sense* of wellbeing. It is about valuing oneself as an individual who teaches. It is about getting to the point of being able to have frank discussions about what is a realistic workload for you, without fear, and it is about how you as an individual might start to think about the role of wellbeing in your life. I sincerely hope that within these pages there is food for thought to nourish and inspire positive change in your life, that will help to transform your day to day life as a teacher. The intention is that the activities and suggestions should be used as a launch for your own, continued explorations into your own wellbeing.

When it comes to wellbeing, we all need to be in it for the longhaul. Gimmicks, short cuts and top tips will come and go, but the habits that will give us an enduring sense of wellbeing and balance in our lives have, in many cases, changed little over millennia, and will require our time, effort and energy. The rewards, even of small changes to our daily lives and routines, can be immense. Teaching is an incredible profession to be a part of. Let's help ourselves, and each other, to thrive.

Go well!

FEATURES OF THIS BOOK

Word clouds: These signpost the key focus of each chapter.

Take 5: These are the five key 'take home' points from each chapter.

Save it for later: Further reading relevant to each chapter.

Try this now: A technique or activity to try aimed at supporting your wellbeing.

Writing it out: A writing prompt to help focus on wellbeing.

NOTE

The information in this book is offered for guidance only and is not intended to be a substitute for the advice of a qualified health care practitioner. It is *always* wise to have concerning symptoms checked out by your primary carer (usually your GP). There are many paths to rebalancing our lives and while there is much we can do in terms of self-help, relevant professionals can also guide and support our progress and offer treatment where appropriate and necessary.

TRY THIS NOW...

Who is your favourite author? When was the last time you enjoyed one of their books? If it has been a while, give yourself the time to read their latest, or reread an old favourite. Even for just 10 minutes a day, you may feel the benefit.

1

WELLBEING MATTERS

BALANCE *Aristotle*
WELLBEING Contentment
DISTRESS
happiness STRESS EUDAIMONIA
EPICURUS

WELLBEING MATTERS

Wellbeing matters. It matters to us personally, socially and economically, and it matters to our communities and our nations. And it has always mattered. How to lead a good life, complete with a sense of wellbeing, has been the focus of philosophers and religions for millennia. While thinkers through the ages have sought to solve the wellbeing and happiness mysteries of their times, the quest for wellbeing will, perhaps, always be a feature of our lives. From Aristotle's proposals about human flourishing, or eudemonic wellbeing, to much more recent research on living a good life (see, for example, the New Economics Foundation's *Five Ways to Wellbeing*), wellbeing clearly matters.

Regardless of the findings of the giants that have gone before us, times change and we must find new ways of seeking balance that help us to thrive in the context in which we find ourselves. That is not to say that wisdom from the past isn't useful for today. Far from it. But we do need to acknowledge the need to interpret, reinterpret and add to it, so that we can give to and gain from the life we have today.

Without a specific focus on wellbeing in our lives, can we live our best lives? Can we achieve what we are fully capable of without self-care? If what we know of wellbeing from thousands of years of thought is anything to go by, the answer to those questions is 'no'.

Interestingly, wellbeing is now an increasingly important consideration of researchers in many fields. According to the European Social Survey wellbeing focus, 'one of the key aims of a democratic government should be to promote the good life: a life which is flourishing, has meaning, and in which people feel happy. In short, a life of high well-being'. Yet the common experience for many is a government that focuses on economic growth ahead of wellbeing. It is no surprise that this does not necessarily lead to a nation awash with wellbeing and happiness.

SAVE IT FOR LATER...

Take a look at the website for the European Social Survey wellbeing focus to find out more about why wellbeing matters and the role it is taking in the work of policymakers and researchers across Europe: **www.esswellbeingmatters.org**. These wellbeing pages summarise research into different aspects of wellbeing and their drivers, as well as explaining two key elements of wellbeing: being happy (the hedonic concept of wellbeing - espoused by Epicurus) and flourishing (the eudemonic concept of wellbeing - put forward by Aristotle).

SAVE IT FOR LATER...

Wellbeing as a philosophical concept has a long history and what is presented here is the briefest of introductions. If you want to explore the best of what has been thought and said about wellbeing from a philosophical perspective, the *Stanford Encyclopaedia of Philosophy* entry on wellbeing is a good place to start, covering theories of wellbeing including hedonism, desire theories, objective list theories and more. Find it here: **www.plato.stanford.edu/entries/well-being**.

You can take your reading further with Aristotle's *Nicomachean Ethics*. Find a copy in any good library or bookshop, or online here: **www.classics.mit.edu/Aristotle/nicomachaen.html**.

DEFINING WELLBEING

Defining wellbeing can be challenging. There is no precise definition shared by all researchers in the field. It is usually taken to mean being in a comfortable, happy or healthy state. But that seems too simplistic for our purposes. When we are experiencing wellbeing, we are feeling good and functioning well. Further than that, though, it is clear that there is a balance to be had between different elements of wellbeing in our lives: biological wellbeing, psychological wellbeing, spiritual wellbeing, our wellbeing at work, and even, or perhaps especially, our social wellbeing – whether our finances are sufficient for our needs, whether we are socially connected with others, whether we feel we are stakeholders in our local communities.

The European Social Survey explains that wellbeing is a multidimensional concept (see **www.esswellbeingmatters.org**). It refers to:

- evaluative wellbeing – how we estimate our lives are going; how happy and satisfied we feel;

- emotional wellbeing – positive day to day feelings, happiness, enjoyment and a lack of depression and anxiety;

- functioning – autonomy, competence, engagement, meaning and purpose, self-esteem, optimism and resilience;

- vitality – sleeping well, feeling energised, able to face life;

- community wellbeing – how we feel about where we live, trust in others, feeling supported, experiencing neighbourliness;

- supportive relationships – feeling that there are people in our lives who support us, offer companionship, and with whom we can discuss intimate matters.

As individuals, we may have other 'wellbeings' that directly impact our lives. It is extremely helpful to appreciate how wellbeing can be categorised in this way. When we do this, it is perhaps more likely that we will be able to rationalise any challenges to our wellbeing that we may be facing. Instead of 'life' being stressful, we can identify more easily which aspect is causing us undue stress. The more specific we are when we reflect on what needs to change in our lives, the more likely we are to be able to make improvements.

Viewing wellbeing as a dynamic process can also be helpful. In *Measuring Our Progress: The Power of Wellbeing* (Abdallah et al., 2011), there is a dynamic model of wellbeing that shows the links between our personal resources (such as health, resilience, optimism and self-esteem), our external conditions (such as work and productivity, income stability and material conditions), our good functioning and the satisfaction of our needs (such as being autonomous, competent, connected to others, safe and secure), and our overall day to day good feelings (happiness, joy, contentment and satisfaction). Other writers and organisations such as Richard Docwra and Life Squared have also highlighted the interconnectedness of different aspects of our wellbeing. Where one dimension of wellbeing is suffering, other dimensions may follow. Where one dimension of wellbeing is strong, other areas that are suffering may be supported. We are complex, interconnected beings.

Writers such as Richard Docwra and Alain de Botton, among others, also go further in their analysis of wellbeing with their perception that modern life might actually be making us ill (see **www.lifesquared.org.uk** and **www.alaindebotton.com**). While many features of life today are highly positive – medical and technological advancements for example – the levels of anxiety and depression felt by many in society indicate that we are struggling. And our inability as a society to provide safe and effective treatment and care for those suffering from poor psychological health is testament to the fact that where we are right now needs urgent attention. Far too many people talk of desperately poor services at times of great crisis in their lives. Wellbeing matters.

SAVE IT FOR LATER...

Life Squared (**www.lifesquared.org.uk**) is a not for profit organisation helping people to live well. The website carries numerous publications on themes such as consumerism, surviving modern life, aging, giving, ethical living, ecological intelligence and much more. The publications are all evidence-informed and free to download. Try *How to be Happy* (**www.lifesquared.org.uk/how-be-happy**) for starters.

Jules Evans' *Politics of Wellbeing* blog explores many dimensions of the concept of wellbeing and is well worth a browse. Find it here: **www.philosophyforlife.org/category/politics-of-well-being**.

WELLBEING MATTERS . . . TO TEACHERS

Wellbeing matters, not just on a practical, societal level – when we are functioning well we are efficient and contributing to society to the best of our abilities – but also (and perhaps more importantly) on a personal level. Wellbeing, however defined by others, is a personal experience. You know when your wellbeing has taken a hit. *You* may not be able to identify precisely what the cause is, or how best to deal with it initially, but the experience remains entirely personal.

Teaching could be considered to be a unique profession in the demands made of its practitioners. While planning and preparation for teaching *may* be completed collaboratively, the actual process of teaching is often undertaken alone. For some this is an isolating experience, particularly if there are behaviour issues to deal with, or an expectation to adhere to behaviour control mechanisms that are ideologically at odds with a teacher's way of working, or if other aspects of the job – expected pedagogy, for example, or assessment and feedback expectations – leave a teacher feeling overwhelmed and unsupported.

Yet the role of educating the next generation is vital in healthy societies and we need teachers to be nurtured in that role. After all, is it possible to safeguard the wellbeing of the young people we teach, if we cannot do that for ourselves? The job can be exhausting – both physically and emotionally draining – and yet also sustaining. It can fill us with the joy and satisfaction of seeing children learn and grow, and it can wipe us of energy and drive. It can bolster wellbeing and destroy it. We simply cannot have teachers working at the pace and depth that many work for the long term without there being devastating consequences for recruitment, retention and the health and wellbeing of the individuals involved.

Wellbeing matters.

CASE STUDY...

It was my first week in my first job as a qualified teacher. A colleague sat next to me in the staff-room and said 'make sure you know how to say no'. I dismissed her comment in my head as a keen and enthusiastic new teacher. Why would I need to say no?! But I've since come to realise that she was telling me that my wellbeing matters and that I may need to equip myself with the language I need to negotiate tasks with my line manager. Saying yes to everything is a short-cut to burnout. Wellbeing is so often about removing stuff from workloads so that what's left can be done more effectively, and without forcing a crisis of wellbeing on teachers who are ill-equipped to deal with the exhausting pressures placed upon them. We have to say no, so that the answer to the important stuff that really will make a difference to children and young people is a resounding yes.

TRY THIS NOW...

What does wellbeing mean to you? How does it manifest in your life? What blocks to wellbeing do you have to negotiate? What would a life characterised by wellbeing look like to you? These prompts may help you to crystallise your personal notion of wellbeing and what it means in your life right now.

TARGETING WELLBEING

The premise of this book is that:

- Wellbeing is a personal matter.

- Workload really matters when it comes to wellbeing. We have to create time for balance.

- Regardless of what the focus is on wellbeing in your school, and the strategies employed for workload reduction, it remains important to focus on *your* wellbeing through the overall balance in your life. Your wellbeing is so much more than your wellbeing at work.

- The numerous evidence-informed strategies for boosting wellbeing can be important in your creation of a balanced life. No, it isn't all about yoga and meditation. But yoga and meditation sure can help!

The more targeted and specific we can be in our quest to raise wellbeing, the more likely we are to create a sustainable sense of balance in our lives.

SAVE IT FOR LATER...

If you want to explore the science of wellbeing further, there are many lines of enquiry to pursue. For example, take a look at the range of wellbeing research at the University of Cambridge's Well Being Institute: **www.psychol.cam.ac.uk/well-being-institute**.

You might also want to explore the work of the Centre for Innovation and Research in Wellbeing at the University of Sussex (**www.sussex.ac.uk/socialwork/cirw**) and Health and Wellbeing Research at the Open University: **www.healthwellbeing.kmi.open.ac.uk**.

Researchers at City, University of London designed a project to assess teachers' work demands and wellbeing on a weekly basis including working weeks and half-term. You can download the *Teacher Wellbeing Research Project* report here: **www.city.ac.uk/__data/assets/ pdf_file/0010/364987/Teacher-Well-Being-Report.pdf**.

SAVE IT FOR LATER...

A Philosophy for the Science of Well-Being by Anna Alexandrova (OUP, 2017) explores tools for philosophy and tools for science when researching wellbeing, and questions such as 'Is there a single concept of wellbeing?' and 'Is there a single theory of wellbeing?'

WRITING IT OUT...

A writing prompt to explore what wellbeing means for you

We all have multiple 'wellbeings', regardless of how the term is defined by different thinkers. What are yours? Wellbeing at home? Wellbeing at work? Wellbeing as a parent? Biological wellbeing? Psychological wellbeing? What would you add? Write a list or paragraph defining your 'wellbeings'. Where are the interconnections? Which areas need your attention most at the moment?

TAKE 5...

- The pursuit of wellbeing has been a feature of life for millennia. Philosophers, theologians and other thinkers through the ages have sought answers to questions of happiness and wellbeing.

- We all have multiple 'wellbeings' that are separate yet interconnected.

- There is a raft of wellbeing research out there from a range of perspectives.

- Wellbeing matters. It matters for teachers as individuals and it matters for communities and societies.

- The creation of a more balanced life for teachers, and anyone, does not rest alone on any one strategy. Wellbeing at work can support our overall wellbeing and vice versa. Workload is key.

2

ALL ABOUT STRESS

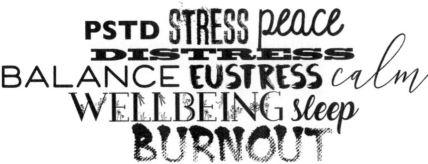

ALL ABOUT STRESS: THE POSITIVE AND THE NEGATIVE

Stress is intrinsic to life. We don't get to travel through the years without encountering its many guises. At times we may be propelled forwards, inspired by our challenging workload and easily able to cope with what comes our way. At other times though, the picture is somewhat different. No matter what, the fact remains that no one gets a free pass. Whether it's work, illness, relationships, living accommodation or any of life's other potential stressors, we will have to face what stress does to us sooner or later.

It is important to note that to do full justice to the theme of stress would require a book far larger than this. Any information and guidance that follows is intended as a starting point. As individuals our stress triggers will vary, as will the strategies we employ to improve our feelings of wellbeing. There is no definitive path to beating excessive stress!

There is an array of research on workplace stress and figures aplenty. But most of us can just take a look around, either at our workplace or our networks on social media and in real life, and see people who are negatively affected. We can also see how wider society is affected, as people grapple with major stressors such as social injustice, poverty and political instability. Even young children speak of being stressed. It's a phenomenon that surrounds us, for obvious reasons.

Having a solid understanding of the landscape of stress is necessary if you're to tackle its negative effects on your life. Using one word – stress – to describe everything from being delayed on public transport to dealing with a sudden death in the family is clearly not constructive or helpful. Understanding the nuances of the term can help us to identify how we are feeling and the point at which motivation becomes something more problematic.

There are several ways of categorising stress. For example, the American Psychological Association (APA) (**www.apa.org**) describes three kinds of stress.

- Acute stress – thrilling in small doses! But can be exhausting if over-done.

- Episodic acute stress – frequent episodes of acute stress. People who take on too much and suffer because of it are thought to experience episodic acute stress.

- Chronic stress – grinding stress that doesn't cease.

There is far more detail on these types of stress on the APA website. For the purposes of starting to understand the nature of any excessive stress that you are feeling, it's worth keeping in mind that there are different kinds of stress, and that there may be more than one source for you.

In the 1950s, Dr Hans Selye made the distinction between *eustress* and *distress*. *Eustress* can be described as good, or positive, stress. The *'eu'* is from the Greek root meaning 'good' (think *eu*phoria). *Distress* can be described as bad, or negative, stress. The *'dis'* is from the Latin root meaning, among others, 'negative' (think *dis*like, *dis*agreement and *dis*belief).

POSITIVE STRESS

Positive stress is what motivates us so that we have the drive to get things done. Without positive stress it is likely that we would underachieve, possibly becoming complacent about our work, and even demotivated.

While positive stress can be demanding, requiring us to apply our talents and skills to the task in hand, we are able to handle these demands. They spur us on without launching us into the excesses of negative stress and the array of biological and psychological symptoms it might cause. Positive stress can be enjoyable, inspiring and deeply satisfying if we have the opportunity to express our creativity and talents in meeting the demands placed on us.

When we are positively stressed we have time to achieve our tasks and goals, and any accountability measures facing us feel fair and appropriate. We may experience challenges, but we have sufficient levels of wellbeing to handle these. Our responses and reactions to events are balanced and there is no chasm between what we are expected to do and what we are able to do.

NEGATIVE STRESS

When the balance in your life between what is realistically achievable and what is currently being demanded of you is off kilter, you risk plunging into negative stress. This is when we no longer feel motivated and the challenges we face are no longer a source of enjoyment and satisfaction. The pressure feels excessive and we do not feel able to cope effectively. When we are in this state, our 'fight or flight' response is heightened and we are more likely to experience the biological and psychological symptoms that are a clear indication that we are under too much stress.

It's important to note that these pressures won't necessarily mean that you won't achieve what you need to achieve. We can be marvellously productive even when our stress levels are well into the negative zone. What we must be aware of, though, is that there is likely to be a cost, biologically, psychologically, or both.

OPTIMUM STRESS

The space between under-stimulation and over-stimulation might be characterised as 'optimum stress'. The point at which stress moves from the positive to the negative will vary for each person and may also vary in the same person over time. When it comes to wellbeing, self-knowledge is a beautiful thing! The more we come to understand how we work, how we respond to the situations life presents us with, and how we seek solutions for any problematic issues we face, the more likely we are to occupy the optimum stress zone. This could ultimately help us to move towards a greater sense of wellbeing than we are currently experiencing.

SYMPTOMS OF NEGATIVE STRESS TO BE AWARE OF

Whether you are experiencing so-called positive or negative stress, your body will be experiencing biological and psychological symptoms. The more alert we can be to this, the greater our chance of modifying behaviour in time so that we can guard against long-term ill-effects.

Symptoms to watch out for include:

- emotional distress – anxiety, panic attacks, volatile moods and mood changes, depression, irritability, anger, tearfulness, sadness;
- tension – headaches, migraines, back pain, and muscular tension;
- digestive problems – heartburn, reflux, irritable bowel syndrome, constipation.

You may also experience:

- raised blood pressure;
- heart palpitations;
- dizziness;
- shortness of breath;
- chest pain;
- eczema;
- ulcers;
- sleep disturbance;
- eating problems – anorexia or over-eating, leading to weight disturbance (loss or gain).

In addition to the symptoms of excessive stress outlined above, there is also the overlying tiredness that excessive stress can cause, which may lead to exhaustion. When your body is exhausted, urgent medical attention is required. The way in which we react to a perceived stressor can have a real and lasting impact on our psychological and biological health.

Many believe that our bodies give us warning signs, with ever increasing urgency, when we are in the thick of excessive stress with no sign of abatement. It may be whispering quietly at first, but if those whispers are ignored, it can only send signals with ever increasing intensity.

When intense or prolonged stress results in debilitating feelings of helplessness, hopelessness and/or worthlessness, an element of depression is involved. Symptoms are frequently also mixed with those of anxiety. Symptoms of depression include:

- depressed mood;
- loss of interest and enjoyment;

- reduced energy leading to fatiguability and diminished activity;

- reduced concentration and attention;

- reduced self-esteem and self-confidence;

- ideas of guilt and unworthiness;

- bleak and pessimistic views of the future;

- ideas or acts of self-harm or suicide;

- disturbed sleep;

- diminished appetite.

Symptoms of anxiety include:

- generalised and persistent anxiety, not restricted to any particular environmental circumstances ('free-floating anxiety');

- worrying excessively;

- feeling nervous or 'on edge';

- trembling;

- muscular tension;

- sweating;

- light-headedness;

- palpitations;

- dizziness;

- abdominal discomfort;

- dry mouth;

- fast pulse rate and/or breathing rate;

- restless fidgeting;

- tension headaches;

- inability to relax;

- frequently seeking assurance.

BURNOUT

If there is no respite from long-term excessive or negative stress, you could experience burnout. When people become burned out either physically or psychologically, they typically have a range of signs and symptoms, including:

- a loss of interest in daily life;

- a diminishing sense of control;

- a loss of a sense of purpose;

- demotivation;

- sleeplessness, or interrupted sleep due to bad dreams or nightmares;

- an inability to concentrate;

- increased dependency on stimulants;

- palpitations and chest pain;

- headaches;

- dizziness.

Burnout is serious. It can hit, seemingly without warning (although there will, or course, have been signs and signals over time that we may not recognise when in the grip of a hectic term) and it requires immediate action with the help of suitably qualified health care practitioners. Your GP will be a good starting point. You may be referred for more specialised treatment.

Helping yourself through work-induced burnout is important. You may find that having a complete break from work, combined with addressing the quality of your sleep, eating healthy food and taking some moderate exercise, are great starting points. Experiencing burnout does not necessarily mean having to leave the teaching profession, or making dramatic changes to your life. It does, however, mean taking time out, returning *only* when your overall health has improved sufficiently, and when any necessary changes to your working patterns are in place.

POST-TRAUMATIC STRESS DISORDER

Post-traumatic stress disorder, or PTSD, has been identified for thousands of years, but has gone under different names over time. PTSDUK (**www.pstduk.org**) explains that some of the previous terms include 'shell-shock' during the First World War, 'war neurosis' during the Second World War and 'combat stress reaction' during the Vietnam War.

PTSDUK defines PTSD as 'essentially a memory filing error caused by a traumatic event'. Such events include serious accidents, bereavement, miscarriage, childhood neglect or prolonged bullying (among many others). During such intensely fearful events, the mind does what it can to survive.

While depression can progress through certain stages, PTSD does not seem to work in this way. Its symptoms can worsen over time if not addressed and may lead to adverse changes in the way in which the brain operates.

You can find out more about PTSD from PTSDUK and other mental health charities such as Rethink Mental Illness (**www.rethink.org**) and Mind (**www.mind. org.uk**).

ADDRESS THE STRESS

There are many other signs indicating a form or degree of stress that is having a potentially damaging impact on you either biologically, psychologically or both. It is vitally important that you get any such symptoms checked out by your GP. If you think that work-related stress may be contributing to your symptoms, it would be helpful for your GP to know.

Stress-related symptoms are often treatable. You may need a combination of rest, relaxation, adjustments in your working practices and possibly even some medication and talking therapy or behavioural treatment, but change for the better is highly possible for most people.

If long-term negative stress goes untreated, the symptoms you experience may become chronic. And let's not be under any illusions here: chronic stress can kill. Research suggests that it could make us more susceptible to heart attack, stroke, and possibly cancer, among other conditions. It really is important to address the stress we feel, especially as a build-up of negative stress may have been occurring for some time before we become fully aware. Self-knowledge is crucial, but we need to allow ourselves the time and space to reflect on how we are feeling, and to seek the most appropriate treatment so that we can return to equilibrium. The key is balance.

CASE STUDY...

I get annoyed when people talk about stress as being all bad. It isn't. I remember reading about good and bad stress when I was training and it made such an impression. I love it when I'm challenged and appropriately stressed. I love it when I get loads done and feel as though I am working really efficiently. But there is a line that's not to be crossed and I am getting better at recognising when I'm overloaded and nearing that line. Spotting it is really a career-long task.

CASE STUDY...

I didn't know that I was about to burn out until I was sitting in the staffroom at the end of the summer term one year and I realised I couldn't really hear what was going on around me. It was just sound. I felt an overwhelming exhaustion. I crawled through to the end of term and then crashed. My energy was at rock bottom and it took months to get back on track. I had worked too hard for too long and I was psychologically and physically beaten. No job should do that to you.

SAVE IT FOR LATER...

The Stress of Life is Hans Selye's famous classic on stress, which still offers useful insights into the nature of stress. You may also want to explore another of his books, *Stress without Distress*. Both are widely available.

SAVE IT FOR LATER...

The latest Education Support Partnership Teacher Wellbeing Index 2018 is available on its website. This index presents a clear picture of the mental health and wellbeing of education professionals in the UK and the ways in which this is changing. This document is well worth a read and will demonstrate clearly that you are not alone in wanting and needing to improve wellbeing and balance. You can find the report here: **www.educationsupportpartnership.org.uk**.

TRY THIS NOW...

William James wrote: *The greatest weapon against stress is our ability to choose one thought over another.* Research, for example from Harvard University, has found that how we respond to stress has important consequences for our functioning, both biological and cognitive. Reframing it so that we *think* about it differently might help us to reach solutions more quickly. When you are facing a stressful situation, or ongoing negative stress, consider these two points:

- What are your thoughts about the stressor?
- What are your thoughts about your ability to cope with and deal with the stressor?

Be aware that what drives our response to negative stress can be subconscious. The more attuned we become, the more likely it is that we can observe our responses and adjust them accordingly.

You may want to keep a record of your responses to stressful events or situations.

TRY THIS NOW...

Think of a time when you experienced positive stress; a time when you felt capable, in control and that you had a good balance in your life overall. What is different now? How far do you feel from that time of balance? Identify one action you can take today to move you closer to that sense of balance.

WRITING IT OUT...

A writing prompt to help you explore what 'stress' means to you

What does the word 'stress' mean to you? Do you associate it with the motivating form of *eustress*? Or is it associated with fear, anxiety or excessive pressure, or *distress*?

Write a paragraph, list or word cloud (whatever works for you) on what you associate with the word 'stress'.

Now think about the converse of this. What characterises the way you feel when you are not under stress?

TAKE 5...

- We all need a certain amount of stress in our lives in order to feel motivated to achieve what we need to achieve. Stress is not all bad!

- There are different kinds of stress that may have multiple sources for you. It is important to understand where any excessive stress you are experiencing is coming from, in order to address it effectively.

- Biological and psychological symptoms of excessive stress must be addressed. It is vitally important to discuss any troubling symptoms with your primary health carer (usually your GP).

- While we talk of biological and psychological symptoms of stress, we must remember that approaches that address issues in a holistic way may be most effective for us. Not every approach will work for everyone, and some strategies can take time to become familiar with.

- The key to addressing stress is to be found in re-establishing *balance* in your life. Solutions do not have to be complicated, but they do need to have balance at their core. Life beyond excessive stress is achievable.

3

STRESS AND TEACHING

Ofsted Accountability
WORKLOAD *MARKING*
STRESS**PREPARATION**
Planning *assessment*

CAUSES OF STRESS IN TEACHING

With the exception of one or two voices, opinion on excessive stress in the teaching profession is virtually unanimous. As a working population, teachers are among the most stressed. And, from what teachers tell us, that stress has an impact on health, relationships and job satisfaction, to name just a few (see research by City, University of London, *Teacher Well-Being Research Project*, July 2017 – **www.city.ac.uk/__ data/assets/pdf_file/0010/364987/Teacher-Well-Being-Report.pdf**).

The Education Support Partnership's recent research into the wellbeing of education professionals in the UK (see *Health Survey 2017* at **www.education supportpartnership.org.uk**) makes the point that while teaching as a profession can offer incredibly high levels of job satisfaction, it is also increasingly pressurised and this is manifestly having a harmful impact on many individuals. In his foreword to the *Health Survey 2017*, Education Support Partnership CEO Julian Stanley states that:

As a society, the need for clear measures that protect the wellbeing and mental health of all has never appeared more urgent. In education it would appear acute. For many of the 1,250 education professionals who responded to this survey, the impact of extremely heavy workloads and rapid change is clearly taking its toll, impacting on the health and the ability of significant numbers to perform at their best, feeding a growing recruitment and retention crisis.

The *Health Survey 2017* brings the reality of teaching life for many teachers into sharp focus. For example:

- 75% of those surveyed said they have faced physical and mental health issues in the last two years because of their work;

- 29% said their job has made them feel stressed most or all of the time (compared with 18% of the UK workforce overall);

- 53% have considered leaving the sector over the past two years as a result of health pressures. For 75%, the main reason given was volume of work and to seek a better work–life balance;

- 50% said they had experienced depression, anxiety or panic attacks due to work. 36% of those who said they experienced problems said they feel it had a negative impact on their students' studies;

- 49% of those who said that they experienced psychological, physical or behavioural problems as a result of work said that their work performance suffered. 47% said that their relationships suffered;

- almost half of respondents felt that their organisation does not support people with mental health problems well;

- 72% of education professionals feel that they do not receive sufficient guidance about their health and wellbeing at work.

Unless a teacher suffering excessive workload expectations and negative stress has access to excellent quality support, the likelihood is that their psychological and biological health may suffer and there may be a knock-on impact on performance at work. Stress can lead to stress, and it requires careful, intelligent and humane handling.

What follows is by no means an exhaustive list of workplace stressors for teachers. These are, however, the issues commonly raised by teachers when discussing their wellbeing at work.

LONG WORKING HOURS

The *Health Survey 2017* revealed that 32% of education professionals work 51+ hours in an average week. Other surveys such as that of the Education Policy Institute (**www.epi.org.uk**) suggest that a significant number of teachers are regularly working more than that with 60 hours a week or more not uncommon. The OECD's *Teaching and Learning International Survey* between 2012 and 2014 (**www.oecd.org/education/school/talis-2013-results.htm**) also found that (secondary) teachers in England work long hours. Longer, in fact, than all but two of the 36 jurisdictions surveyed. Significantly, the extra time spent working did not necessarily equate to more time for teaching. Rather, it was taken up with marking and administrative tasks.

If long working hours are adversely impacting your wellbeing as a teacher, raise the issue with your line manager, your GP, the Education Support Partnership and, if necessary, your union.

WORKLOAD

Strongly linked to long working hours is the overall workload of teachers. There is no doubt that the planning and preparation of new resources, lesson plans and schemes of work, not to mention assessment and marking, contributes tremendously to the workload of teachers.

Excessive workload is linked to a worsening of wellbeing and imbalance in the lives of teachers. The *Health Survey 2017* revealed that 77% of those experiencing poor mental health in connection with work said that excessive workload could be a cause.

ACCOUNTABILITY

Linked to workload are accountability demands. There are many ways in which teachers are held accountable for their work. While the vast majority would say they have no problem with the concept of accountability, there can be some reticence about OFSTED.

It is fair to say that OFSTED has put considerable effort into mythbusting and generally being available and accessible so that teachers' questions and concerns about inspection can be addressed quickly. At the time of writing, OFSTED's National Director, Education is active on Twitter responding quickly to questions raised. It is worth following the person with this role to glean valuable insights into inspection.

If OFSTED visits your school, it should not be a stressful event. If it is, something is wrong. It should simply be a matter of demonstrating to inspectors how successfully you work with your children to achieve the best for them using the evidence you have. The Department for Education poster, *Reducing Teacher Workload* (available to download from **www.gov.uk**) makes it clear that OFSTED (relevant at the time of writing):

- does not expect to see any specific amount of marking and feedback. It says that this is for each school to decide through its assessment policy;

- does not expect to see a written record of oral feedback (but you will need to show how oral and written feedback promotes learning);

- does not specify how planning should be set out (including the degree of detail it contains);

- does not require lesson plans to be made available to inspectors;

- does not expect a specific format for pupil tracking information;

- does not expect to see evidence of the monitoring of teaching and learning above and beyond what the school uses routinely.

There is a substantial amount of information available on the OFSTED website about what is and is not expected during an OFSTED inspection. There are also numerous books and blog posts available that have been written about OFSTED. The bottom line, though, is that if OFSTED hangs over your school like the threat of impending doom, it could be that you need to extract yourself from such drama and focus on the latest information about what an inspection should and should not entail. That's not to say that some schools don't experience traumatic inspections – some do, and there is no benefit in denying that – but there are channels through which to complain if necessary. For many, inspection is a beneficial and even positive experience.

If you are experiencing undue pressure as a result of internal accountability procedures, it would be worth talking to your local union representative to help determine whether what you are experiencing is acceptable or not. If necessary, change can be brought about through discussion on a local level once senior leaders know that the impact of expectations is negative. This is why good channels of communication between senior leaders and those representing teachers is crucial. Communication between teacher governors and the remainder of the staff helps too.

If you raise concerns through the appropriate channels and you feel that they have not been handled effectively enough as to bring about positive change, you may wish to speak to someone else at your union (perhaps a national officer) or the Education Support Partnership for further advice on your next moves.

Undue accountability pressures can wreck careers if unchecked. Always raise concerns if you need to sooner rather than later, and pursue them until you feel the path ahead is fair and achievable.

A LACK OF BALANCE IN LIFE

A balanced life for a teacher is one in which working life does not obliterate every other aspect of life. Work is contained within the hours it should take, and does not encroach on time that should be reserved for the rest of your life. And yet the Education Support Partnership *Health Survey 2017* found that 45% of respondents did not achieve the right balance between their home lives and their working lives. For 74% of respondents with poor mental health as a result of problems at work, this lack of balance was thought to be a cause.

While work–life balance seems to be such an unhelpful term – if we cannot even bring ourselves to think of work as a time when we are *living* we really need a change of career – we do need to find *balance*. Too much of anything distorts our experience of life, and overwork can kill. Research published in the *Lancet* in 2015 found that 'employees who work long hours have a higher risk of stroke than those working standard hours' (see **www.thelancet.com/journals/lancet/article/ PIIS0140-6736(15)60295-1/fulltext**). We know that teachers work long hours. Some work excessively long hours. This has a direct impact on the sense of balance felt and consequently on the negative or excessive stress experienced.

The need for balance in our lives cannot be over stated.

DEMANDS ON TIME

For 45% of respondents to the *Health Survey 2017* who described their mental health as poor as a result of work pressures, unreasonable demands from their manager is a cause. Not only are teachers struggling under the weight of workload demands, but the expectations to achieve too tight deadlines or to squeeze too much into the time available are also huge drains on wellbeing. Unless there is excellent support for time management and workload reduction, teachers have to face the pressure of not being able to meet the expectations made of them. Breakdown or burnout become real possibilities for teachers in this position.

RAPID PACE OF CHANGE

The pace of change in education, for example curriculum changes and expectations, accountability changes and pedagogical changes, is cited in the *Health Survey 2017* by 44% of those experiencing poor mental health in connection with work. The relative lack of stability in education can have a dramatic impact on wellbeing at work for teachers who must respond to ever-changing demands.

OTHER CAUSES OF STRESS IN TEACHING

To lesser extents, income levels, students' behaviour, redundancy and restructuring, workplace bullying by colleagues, problems with students' parents, discrimination and retirement all factor in causes of poor mental health for teachers.

All contributing factors to poor wellbeing at work can lead to work bleeding into weekends, evenings and holidays, neglecting family and friends, avoiding family commitments and being unable to switch off sufficiently as to gain benefit from time away from work.

PSYCHOLOGICAL AND BIOLOGICAL HEALTH ISSUES

The vicious cycle between excessive stress and ill health is well documented. Stress can bring on unwanted symptoms. In the *Health Survey 2017* 56% of respondents experienced behavioural symptoms such as changes to appetite and mood swings, 50% experienced physical symptoms such as raised blood pressure, muscle tension, headaches and migraines, and 50% experienced psychological symptoms such as depression, anxiety and panic attacks. Just 23% experienced no such symptoms. In turn, these symptoms can make working efficiently and effectively almost impossible and consequently, symptoms of negative stress can worsen.

FATIGUE

Research (see the City, University of London, *Teacher Well-Being Research Project*) suggests that teachers need their half-term breaks. There is a statistically significant drop in fatigue levels during half-term breaks that continues to an extent after returning to work, indicating that teachers retain some of the benefits of having a break for some time after that break. It also tells us that for at least part of a term, teachers are working in a fatigued state, to a greater or lesser extent. And while stress can make us feel fatigued, fatigue can certainly worsen our stress.

CASE STUDY...

I was really struggling to work collaboratively with my head of department. He was never available, didn't respond to emails and when I asked him about my concerns about a pupil he just didn't get back to me. When I could finally ask him face to face he responded with 'well he's OK for me'. That's not OK. That's not even mildly acceptable. I get that he was stressed, but his not dealing with it meant that his stress became my stress. It was very damaging to our working relationship. In the end I confronted him about it. We cleared the air, which was great, but it is so important not to let colleagues get away with that kind of behaviour. As a department, we have made sources of support for stress more visible and we now talk about it at our departmental meetings. This has helped us not only to deal with unnecessary stress as it arises but to prevent it from happening too.

WRITING IT OUT...

A writing prompt to encourage the identification of stressors

The effects of negative stress can hit without us being able to determine precisely what it is that is causing us most grief. It helps to identify, and isolate, stressors as they arise. Writing them down can help us to firm up our plans to resolve them. What are your most pressing stressors? What steps can you take towards resolving them? (Remember, you do not need to write an essay. Just a few words or sentences will do.)

SAVE IT FOR LATER...

While these pages explore some of the causes of stress in the teaching profession, it also pays to be mindful of the other causes of stress that can affect us all. The Mind website has useful information on more general causes of stress in our lives: **www.mind.org.uk**.

TRY THIS NOW...

A lack of balance in life is a strong factor in the degree of wellbeing we are able to achieve. How balanced does your life feel today? If you could create ideal circumstances, what would balance look like in your life?

TAKE 5...

- There are numerous causes of stress in teaching. Some are shared experiences for many in the profession. Others are more specific to individuals and the schools they work in.

- Workload remains a significant cause of excessive stress in the teaching profession. When we address workload, we also address negative stress.

- Long working hours and unreasonable demands also feature strongly in causes of excessive stress for teachers.

- Surveys on teacher stress can give us valuable insights into what must change in order to support teacher wellbeing. But we must be mindful of our own stressors, which may not feature in such surveys.

- Teacher wellbeing is affected by a wide range of issues in schools. If your wellbeing is adversely affected, you are far from alone.

4

MAKING STRESS WORK FOR YOU

DEADLINES **GOALS** STRESS
PRIORITISATION STRESS
NO! POSITIVES
Communication Assumptions
Pareto principle

CAN STRESS WORK?

Let us be entirely realistic here. Stress *can* work for us. And we *can* use it as a motivator to making much needed changes or rising to the challenge. But stress also kills. And the line between the good stuff and the bad may be imperceptible. Making the most of stress before it tips us into distress is dependent on us knowing where to draw the line. We can be supported in this – coaxed and nurtured – but ultimately we must decide alone where our limits are. Keep that in mind. If in doubt, stop. Your life is worth more than whatever may be your current stressors. Taking time out to focus on preventing negative stress from taking hold is always wise.

On the assumption that you are on the motivating side of the line, these suggestions for making stress work for you may help.

WISE GOALS

Whether you are setting life goals or daily goals, there are a few key ideas to keep in mind.

- Be utterly realistic. It is far better to accomplish goals than set yourself such high targets that you can only fail. Being realistic does not imply under-achievement. It simply suggests that you strive in a way that is not going to wreck your health!

- Make sure that your goals are motivating. If you are not inspired by them, then don't expect yourself to commit to them.

- In setting your goals, use the impetus and drive that the positive stress is giving you. Utilise that sense of urgency.

- Be as specific as you can about what you are seeking to achieve. Set time limits.

- Create goals that have definable end points so that it is clear when you have achieved them.

- Find a way to record your goals that works well for you. Bullet journals are very popular (take a look at Pinterest for ideas). Writing goals down helps to clarify your intention.

- Reflect on goals achieved and goals yet to be achieved. Ditch any that no longer serve you.

- Use this habit of crafting and recording goals to refine your direction each day.

RUTHLESS PRIORITISATION

Teachers under pressure have to be ruthless over what gets attention. And while we cannot really *manage* time – it passes at the same rate each day regardless of our interventions – we can learn to ration our efforts and energy according to the time we have available to us. Crucial, when every day is overloaded.

Once again, the importance of knowing your capabilities and limits (we all have them, it is nothing negative) is key. Some thoughts:

- Look at the time you have available and the tasks you must complete. Now consider your energy levels and motivation and allocate time accordingly. Be ruthless. Aside from the stuff that *has* to be done, choose what is important and effective.

- Be mindful of deadlines. Missing them can add to the stress of others, but they must be set realistically. If you have deadlines that go beyond reasonable expectations, speak up. They should be changed for something more realistic, or the expectations of the task reduced.

- The chances are, your most effective productivity happens in short bursts. Does that apply to you? If so, really try to notice when your peak effort should happen. To some degree this is irrelevant for teachers due to the enforced nature of the timetable, but all the spaces between are yours to manipulate for your benefit.

- Allocate time to recharge so that your effectiveness is heightened on your return to work. Move around, eat and drink something, talk to someone, go outside, do some stretches – whatever works for you.

- Divide tasks up if they are too unwieldy for the time available. This way you will at least make a start and reduce the magnitude of what needs to be done.

- Limit your choices where possible on tasks that do not require a definitive response.

- If procrastination is affecting your completion of a task, do something else that will grab your attention. There is no point persevering with a task that does not have your attention unless absolutely vital.

- Aim to complete one task at a time. Not always possible as a teacher, but research does seem to suggest that is best. Divided attention can lead to tension.

PARETO PRINCIPLE

The Pareto principle, also known as the 80/20 rule, holds that for much of what we do roughly 80% of the effects come from 20% of the causes. In other words, for a significant amount of our days, we are not that productive! So if we get 80% of our results from 20% of our effort, why not be strategic about our task list to make sure that we prioritise the effort that brings about more effect, at a time of the day when we are most productive? Only you can determine the details!

TRY THIS NOW...

Plan a day based on the Pareto principle. Reflect on how easy it was to organise, how it felt to work through that day, whether it released time for you, whether you would try it again, what changes you would make.

BEING 'GOOD ENOUGH'

Being inspired by stress so that we really make it work for us is in part dependent on our ability to know when to stop working on something because we have done enough for what is required. Many teachers go above and beyond the call of duty, and that is excellent if they are not *obliged* to and it does not adversely affect their wellbeing. But for most of the time, good enough really is good enough. (With apologies to D.W. Winnicott.)

We can make this idea work for us when life is overloaded if we banish all ideas of perfectionism (see page 54). If there is an expectation of delivering more than is realistic, conversations need to be had.

'Good enough' can work really well and help us to manage overloaded schedules, but it is worth being aware that it *can* be a source of stress in itself. If the demands placed on us are such that we end up feeling everything we do could be better, we may find wellbeing at work suffers. Again, if this resonates with you, it is time to talk about workload (see Chapter 5).

SAYING 'NO'

Great communication is a key tactic in the quest to control stress. We cannot survive in a profession with such loose workload boundaries unless we are proficient at saying 'no'. You probably notice that you have some colleagues who have a natural skill when it comes to refusing tasks, while others agree to everything and worry later about how to fit it all in. No guesses for who is the least stressed between the two!

Saying 'no' does not need to be confrontational. Neither does it need inordinately long explanations. If you are already operating at optimum levels, then simply absorbing all new tasks that come your way would certainly adversely impact your wellbeing and balance. You need to maintain your positive stress without straying into overload. These ideas may help:

- If a task is not your job, say no. If you take on the work of others, you will not be able to complete your own work to the best of your ability.

- If a task is not a job you want to work towards doing in the future, say no. It can be hugely beneficial to take on tasks that offer the opportunity to learn a new role or prepare for a promotion *if* time allows. This may sound ruthless, but if the additional task you are being asked to do offers no such benefits, it is best not to take it on.

- If you see no beneficial value to the task, for either you as a teacher or the pupils you teach, say no. Or at least, raise your concerns. It would be wise to discuss your thoughts with whoever is handing down the task, but if there is no benefit to it, common sense dictates it should go.

- If you have philosophical objections to the task, say no. Obviously this needs clarification, but your reasons should be heard.

SAVE IT FOR LATER...

Brush up on assertiveness skills if you feel you need some help making yourself heard or expressing yourself. The Mayo Clinic website offers extensive advice on a wide range of symptoms and conditions as well as healthy lifestyles. The advice there on developing assertiveness is a great place to start: **www.mayoclinic.org**.

TAKING TIME OUT

However skilled we are at seeking to make stress work for us, there may come a time when time out is the only way ahead. When the pressures of the job tip the balance and become a negative experience, and when biological and psychological symptoms cause us distress, we have to listen and to stop. Taking time out sooner rather than later is invariably the wise response.

If the leave you take becomes extended you will need to see your GP and may want to ask for advice from your union or the Education Support Partnership. These people and organisations are here to help you so use their skills and expertise. You do not have to feel alone.

FACING UP

There may be times in our careers when, despite making the most of things, doing what we can to improve the way we feel, seeking to make stress work for us, and taking what steps we can to manage workload, we would be better off with a change.

Facing up to the need for change can be incredibly liberating. There is no prize for longevity at a particular school if the culture and ethos simply does not work for you. While the temptation is often to leave the profession altogether, it is definitely worth considering changing school initially. Schools vary so much in the opportunities for wellbeing that they afford their staff members. It could be that the perfect school is out there for you, and you can reset your career in a more supportive environment.

It may be, however, that it really is time to move on to something else entirely. That is not an easy decision to make, and only you can make it, but no decision needs to be permanent. There is always the possibility of a return to teaching in a more appropriate school if that suits you, and the experience you gain in the interim is bound to serve you well.

If a permanent move from teaching is for you, just take a moment to identify some of the key skills and expertise you developed at the chalkface. No experience is ever wasted! Let the situation you find yourself in now be the impetus for the change you need. Stress *can* work for the good.

CASE STUDY...

I'm not a natural at deadlines. I tend to do things at the last minute because I *have* to do them. In a career like teaching that can be really stressful for me and for others relying on me. So I create false deadlines ahead of the true deadline. It works for me! I have also tried to make sure that I cram as much as possible into the hours before the pupils arrive in the morning. It means getting into school quite early, but that is when I work best. I have tried cramming loads into my evenings but it just does not work for me. It makes sense to work to my strengths!

WRITING IT OUT...

A writing prompt to explore your ideal work situation

Imagine you are in your perfect working environment. Where are you working? What role do you have? How pressured do you feel? How much do you enjoy your work? Now consider the differences between your ideal working environment and where you find yourself now. Is change indicated? Can you make those changes in your current employment?

TAKE 5...

- Stress can kill. We can make it work for us if our circumstances allow that, but we should never underestimate how serious negative stress and the inevitable impact on wellbeing can be.

(Continued)

(Continued)

- The way we allocate time is crucial in safeguarding our wellbeing. We should aim to bo wise about working when we are more energised.

- Perfection is impossible, so 'good enough' is fine.

- Take time out if necessary. You may save your teaching career or decide that another direction would benefit you right now. Either way, your wellbeing must come first. We are so much more than our job titles.

- If it has not been possible to make the stress you feel in your job work for you, it may be time to move on, either to a different school or out of the profession altogether.

5

ASKING FOR HELP

GRANTS *friendship* **psychotherapy** **SUPPORT** colleagues *Nurturing* helplines **NHS** STRESS *Counselling*

ADMIT THAT YOU ARE STRUGGLING

Excessive stress is a bad thing. That's indisputable. But the process of dealing with excessive stress and emerging the other side somewhat changed *can* be a positive experience. And it is probably fair to say that we are more likely to reap any positive benefits if we ask for help. In fact, we could go as far as to say that one of the few features common to most people who successfully emerge from a period of excessive stress is that they asked for help.

However, it is a sad fact of life that many of us do not like to admit that we are struggling. Perhaps we'd rather not ask for help. And while we may offer help to other people, it is fair to say that this can be in the expectation that our offers won't be taken up. It is possible that we feel we should be able to cope alone, or that there is some shame in saying 'I cannot deal with this, please help'. Whatever the reasons, we need to put those thoughts to one side and seek the assistance that will help us to build a greater sense of balance in our lives.

Research completed on behalf of the Education Support Partnership (see *Health Survey 2017: The mental health and wellbeing of education professionals in the UK –* **www.educationsupportpartnership.org.uk**) found that 72% of those surveyed felt their organisation didn't provide them with sufficient guidance on health and wellbeing, with 32% reporting that they were not able to access any type of mental health support at work. Evidently, we have a problem.

Once you acknowledge that you could do with some help, knowing where to turn for timely and appropriate support is essential for all teachers. Some suggestions follow; use them to inspire your next steps.

NHS

While it can be a good idea to back away from Dr Google, so as not to be convinced that your benign symptom may be a sign of something far more serious, the internet can be an excellent source of support and signposting. Just take great care over the websites that you consult.

The NHS website (**www.nhs.uk**) is the UK's largest health website, and the official website of the NHS. There, you will find a 'Health A-Z' about a vast range of conditions and treatments. At the time of writing, the most common conditions searched were stomach ache, depression, diabetes, chest infection and back pain. Just enter your symptoms to access information on possible treatments and next steps. The information is checked regularly so you can feel confident that you are getting the latest advice.

The NHS website is not intended to be a replacement for a consultation with the relevant health care practitioner. Rather, it is a source of information to help you to determine what your next steps should be in moving towards a healthier and happier version of you.

GP

In the UK, your GP is your primary health carer. He or she would usually be your first port of call for any health concerns. Many health issues can be handled by your GP, but in the event of needing more specialised input, your GP can refer you to the relevant practitioners.

Most GPs do not claim to be experts on mental health issues, so if you think that your symptoms would be better managed by a mental health expert, ask for a referral.

It can be wise to find out as much as you can about the services and support that are available in your area. This varies around the country, so before any appointments with your GP, do some research and ask specifically for any service or support that you think would be particularly beneficial for you.

It's important that your GP has the full picture of what you are experiencing both psychologically and biologically. If you feel that excessive workplace stress may be a contributing factor, tell him/her and it can be recorded in your notes. Being completely honest with your GP, however hard it might be to open up, will also help him/her to target the next steps more effectively.

While we would hope that every trip to see a GP results in a plan of appropriate action to help us move towards better health and wellbeing, that is not always the case. If you feel that your consultation with your GP has not been beneficial, you can request to see a different GP. Do not give up. Appropriate help will be out there. It is a matter of finding someone who you can work with collaboratively to move you on into a place of greater wellbeing.

HEALTH INSURANCE SCHEMES

Some health insurance schemes offer telephone access to a GP. For example, Benenden Health (**www.benenden.co.uk**) offers a wide range of benefits to members including 24/7 access to a GP and a psychological wellbeing helpline, and at £10.50 per month (at the time of writing) is affordable for many. Other health insurance schemes exist.

Such helplines can be incredibly effective in helping you to work through your immediate concerns, and determine a plan of action for the longer term. They can signpost you to services in your area and help you to feel supported as you work towards a greater sense of balance in your life.

PRIVATE THERAPISTS

It is always important to discuss any psychological and biological health concerns you have with your GP, but you may also decide to seek out counselling or psychotherapy on a private basis. If you take this path, it is important to ensure that the therapist you select is part of a professional body which expects certain professional standards (including a complaints process that ensures any complaints are effectively handled).

The British Association for Counselling and Psychotherapy is a professional association for the counselling professions in the UK. There is information and a therapist directory on the website: **www.bacp.co.uk**.

The UK Council for Psychotherapy is another organisation concerned with psycho-therapists and psychotherapeutic counsellors in the UK. You can find a therapist on the website: **www.psychotherapy.org**.

LINE MANAGER

Your line manager should be in a position to help if you are struggling with excessive stress that is destroying your wellbeing. We all have a responsibility to communicate workplace difficulties to those in a position to bring about improve-ments. After all, if we say nothing, nothing will be done.

Effective management should facilitate discussions about general wellbeing at work. In other words, if those managing you are doing their jobs well, they will have a pretty good idea about whether your workload is a source of positive or neg-ative stress for you. That said, when in the thick of a hectic term, even the most astute line managers may miss the signs that a colleague is struggling.

If you need to have a frank discussion with your manager about how work is for you right now, do not attempt to do this without setting aside uninterrupted time. This will usually mean making an appointment to talk. Plan what you need to say, and do not leave the most important stuff until last. Timely action can greatly reduce your risk of suffering adversely when negative stress takes hold, so do not delay.

If you feel that discussing your workload with your line manager may not be such a wise idea, just remember that each time teachers are surveyed about their men-tal health, results show shockingly high numbers of people suffering. The *Health Survey 2017* published by the Education Support Partnership is a case in point (you can read this here: **www.educationsupportpartnership.org.uk/resources/research-reports/2017-health-survey**). You are not alone. And it would be helpful if we could all trust that our concerns will be taken seriously with no detrimental impact on our work and careers.

TRUSTED COLLEAGUES

While your line manager may well be in a position to actually *do* something about your workload and experiences at work to help ease the negative stress you may be experiencing, other trusted colleagues may also be able to help. It can often be the case that we don't *know* what help may be out there among colleagues because we don't know what the skills pool is among staff and do not particularly want to be the one to say 'who can help me?' But the fact is that the more we talk about the difficulties we face at work in the spirit of openness and the desire for balance, the more likely we are to find solutions.

It is fair to say that an open and supportive culture in a school takes constant nurturing, so speaking up about the ways in which we might best tackle issues that negatively impact wellbeing is important. You will soon discover who feels the same among your colleagues and together you may be more effective at bringing about positive change.

UNIONS

Teacher unions have long been working hard to support teachers in the quest to improve their wellbeing. They typically offer professional development sessions on teacher wellbeing and these can usually be easily accessed. Some offer articles and guidance on dealing with excessive stress and working towards greater balance in your life and you may have access to a helpline for stress-related issues.

If you do not belong to a union, take a look at their websites to see whether what they offer might support your wellbeing. There is a full list of UK teacher unions on Wikipedia, but these two are a good place to start for classroom teachers:

NASUWT: **www.nasuwt.org.uk**

NEU: **www.neu.org.uk**

The local union representatives can offer members support, guidance and advice where appropriate, so if you are a member of a union, make sure you know who to speak to in your school or locality.

EDUCATION SUPPORT PARTNERSHIP

As the UK's only charity providing mental health and wellbeing support services to all education staff and organisations, the Education Support Partnership offers a vast range of support for teachers in need and is an incredibly helpful resource. It is worth taking a good look at the website (**www.educationsupportpartnership. org.uk**) for their full offer but here is a selection:

- telephone support and counselling;
- email support and live chat;
- grants for those in genuine financial need;

- training and development fund;
- information and advice.

The support from Education Support Partnership is absolutely targeted to the needs of those working in the teaching profession and is invaluable for many. Try not to wait until stresses and anxieties have built up to unmanageable levels before finding out how they can help you.

CHARTERED COLLEGE OF TEACHING

Although in its very early days, the Chartered College of Teaching seeks to support the work of teachers, and wellbeing is integral to that. Take a look at **www.char tered.college** for further information.

NATIONAL CHARITIES CONCERNED WITH MENTAL HEALTH

There are many charities that offer support for people suffering from excessive stress. Many offer confidential support lines or extensive information and advice online. An internet search will identify those most helpful to you. Here are some to start with:

- Rethink Mental Illness: **www.rethink.org**
- Heads Together: **www.headstogether.org.uk**
- Time to Change: **www.time-to-change.org.uk**
- Mind: **www.mind.org.uk**
- Mental Health UK: **www.mentalhealth-uk.org**
- Mental Health Foundation: **www.mentalhealth.org.uk**
- Sane: **www.sane.org.uk**
- Together for Mental Wellbeing: **www.together-uk.org**
- Centre for Mental Health: **www.centreformentalhealth.org.uk**

SELF-HELP GROUPS

Self-help groups tend to emerge out of need and can be readily accessed in communities both real and virtual. While it is always wise to exercise caution when seeking advice and support from any kind of group, those that exist to further understanding about particular conditions and the treatments available can be tremendously helpful for people affected. An internet search is a great place to start. Word of mouth is also helpful in determining possible sources of advice and support.

SOCIAL MEDIA

Love it or hate it, social media is a pretty efficient way of connecting with other people who may be experiencing the same as you. And when connections take place, so too do discussions of mutually shared experiences and potential solutions.

If you're new to social media, it is worth knowing that there is a relatively large teacher population on Twitter. While there can on occasion be quite fiery 'debates' about various issues in education (not so great for wellbeing!), there are also many teachers willing to help, share ideas and generally be a force for good in the profession. Look out for relevant hashtags (you can search on the site via hashtags that help you to access relevant threads and themes) and follow any tweeters who interest you.

There are also many teaching-related Facebook pages, and Pinterest offers ideas aplenty if you need to streamline planning or simply want some fresh input.

The trick to making social media work for you is to be disciplined in how you use it. Curate who you follow carefully, or have different accounts for different aspects of your life, and also follow the social media policies of your school and union. Many teachers keep clear boundaries between private use (for friends and family) and professional use. You may also want to consider taking a break from social media use if ever it is impeding your overall wellbeing. Many prolific users of social media take complete breaks from it on a regular basis.

FAMILY AND FRIENDS

Family and friends can be the first to notice that we are struggling and sometimes the last to whom we will listen! If those close to you are noticing that you are not your usual self, listen to what they have to say. And if you could really do with some slack, reach out for support if at all possible. Talk about what's going on for you so that your nearest and dearest do not have to second guess your mood. Relationships are all about give and take so if this is a time when you need more from others, there is bound to be a time in the future when the favour can be returned.

SAMARITANS

The Samaritans offers a safe place to talk about whatever is causing you distress. You do not have to be suicidal to call. Trained staff are available 24 hours a day, 365 days a year. You can call, email, visit or write to the Samaritans.

www.samaritans.org

Call 116 123 (UK)

Welsh Language Line: 0808 164 0123

Email: **jo@samaritans.org**

Write: Freepost RSRB-KKBY-CYJK, PO Box 9090, Stirling, FK8 2SA

You can find your nearest branch to visit on the website.

The Samaritans also has a presence on social media sites such as Twitter and Facebook.

YOUR BANK

If your concerns are financial, your union and the Education Support Partnership may be able to offer guidance on what to do next. Your bank is also an important port of call. Money plays a key role in wellbeing so it is important not to let concerns rumble on without seeking support if necessary. The Money Charity may also be a source of help: **www.themoneycharity.org.uk**.

WRITING IT OUT...

A writing prompt to explore the support most beneficial to you

Was there a time in the past when you needed and received support? If so, what worked well for you? Being able to talk to someone? Perhaps the process of writing out your anxieties helps you to deal with them? Having an advocate help to resolve an issue? Take a moment to consider and write down what kind of support suits you best.

CASE STUDY...

My head caught up with me in the corridor one day and asked me how I was. 'Not great' was all I could muster. He started talking about how difficult he had found his first year of teaching. He talked about struggles I didn't think someone like him would ever have had. I cried, but he was very understanding. He got me a cup of tea and asked me what he could do to help. It was the best thing anyone could have said to me. In fact, I think it's one of the most important things any manager can ever say, and I plan to say it as much as I can throughout my teaching career.

TRY THIS NOW...

Everyone needs a 'team' for support, and yet at times when the pressure is high, it is easy to forget to reach out for help, or to feel that even if we reached out, no support would be forthcoming. Spend a few moments now making a list of the people and organisations that you could turn to should you ever need to. Keep this list somewhere accessible. At times when we are really in need, knowing where to turn can be invaluable.

SAVE IT FOR LATER...

The Mental Health Foundation has produced a booklet about the health benefits of altruism. While no-one would suggest that it's wise to help others at the expense of your own mental health and wellbeing, there is most certainly a balance to be had. This guide explores the evidence that doing good does you good and invites the reader to keep track of altruistic acts to see whether they are having a positive impact on your life. Download the booklet here: **www.mentalhealth.org.uk/publications/doing-good-does-you-good**.

TAKE 5...

- If help is offered, don't be afraid to take it. Collaborations can ease workloads, even if these are temporary.

- If you see a colleague struggling, offer help. Follow up in a few days, too. As the Mental Health Foundation research found, 'Doing Good Does You Good'.

- You do not have to suffer alone. There are many sources of help, support and advice out there. Seek it out sooner rather than later.

- Take care when seeking support that it comes from a reputable organisation or someone with relevant credentials.

- Creating a list of potential sources of support can ease stress in times of need. Change is possible.

6

STRATEGIES FOR EVERY DAY

First aid HONESTY
COLLABORATION
discussion

THE EVERY DAY

Think of this chapter as a first aid cabinet. Nothing within it *alone* can make a dramatic difference to your life, but taken as part of a wider focus on your wellbeing needs may see you though to a greater sense of equilibrium and the impetus to tackle some of the deeper causes of stress in your working life. That's not to dismiss the use and value of these ideas, however. Mental health first aid can save careers. It's as simple as that. Whether instigated by your school or by you, timely interventions can be the difference between long-term overwhelm and recovery, and between leaving the profession and remaining.

The suggestions below are loosely divided into strategies at school level and strategies at an individual level although there is an obvious cross-over between these two categories. The ideas here are by no means exhaustive, but may suit you and your school context. They may also serve as a launch for your own explorations into what helps you to feel better through the challenges of your working day. Some can be achieved relatively easily, and others will require collaboration and discussion within your school community.

You may also wish to explore the ideas in Chapter 9, Maintaining Balance, to use alongside those below where appropriate.

SCHOOL-LEVEL

These ideas may help to keep wellbeing at the heart of your school's operations:

A FORUM FOR THE HONEST DISCUSSION OF ISSUES CAUSING STRESS

Keeping the discussion going about stress and wellbeing experienced by teachers is essential in schools. And we all share in the responsibility for that process, as both listeners and speakers. An ideal set-up would be space and time to articulate matters that are impacting on your wellbeing at work. This could be a regular slot on the agenda of staff meetings, a method for feeding back to relevant staff members anonymously, ad hoc discussions on wellbeing as and when the need arises, wellbeing buddies – there are numerous possibilities. The keys to making this work are maintaining the forum so that its importance or relevance in your school does not slip, making sure that discussions are undertaken in the spirit of mutual vulnerability, with no fear of damaging consequences, and committing to finding a path ahead for resolving the unnecessary stress.

Such a forum does not need to be excessively time consuming. This is about raising and discussing concerns in a timely manner so that rising stress does not become exploding stress. Done well, this improves communication in the school more generally, and should certainly help teachers to develop skills as reflective practitioners edging towards ways of working that are more sustaining of a healthy and balanced life. While some issues raised will undoubtedly require action, other times the conversation had may suffice.

ASSESSMENT, PLANNING, MARKING AND FEEDBACK THAT WORKS IN YOUR CONTEXT FOR YOUR PUPILS

The assessment, marking and feedback expectations that are made of teachers vary significantly from school to school and phase to phase. Too often, debates about this key aspect of teaching focus too heavily on one age group or another without considering far wider implications. This can lead to pronouncements that some practice or other is *the* way forward and will work *everywhere* for *everyone*. Evidently this is not the case.

There is no doubt that this dimension of your working life will need to be closely scrutinised if you are to achieve your goal of improved balance and wellbeing in your life. But this should ideally be done in collaboration with colleagues and with specific reference to the needs of you as a teacher and your pupils as learners. This is where the overall ethos of your school and of the senior leadership team will heavily influence how inclusively such a process is undertaken.

There are some texts to support the refinement of assessment, planning, marking and feedback in your school. Some starting points are here:

- *Eliminating Unnecessary Workload around Marking: Report of the Independent Teacher Workload Review Group*, Department for Education, 2016 (available to download online);

- The *Making Every Lesson Count* series published by Crown House Publishing;

- *Mark. Plan. Teach,* Ross Morrison McGill, Bloomsbury Education, 2017 (see *Save It for Later* below);

- *100 Ideas for Early Years Practitioners: Observation, Assessment and Planning,* Marianne Sargent, Bloomsbury Education, 2018;

- *Teaching Four and Five Year Olds: The Hundred Review of the Reception Year in England* (available on the Early Excellence website: **www.earlyexcellence. com**);

- *Teaching and Learning Toolkit*, Education Endowment Foundation (available online at **www.educationendowmentfoundation.org.uk/evidence-summaries/teaching-learning-toolkit/#closeSignup**);

- *Making Good Progress: The Future of Assessment for Learning,* Daisy Christodoulou, OUP, 2017;

- *Lean Lesson Planning: A Practical Approach to Doing Less and Achieving More in the Classroom*, Peps Mccrea (CreateSpace Independent Publishing Platform, 2015).

All of that said, some generic ideas to consider include:

- Whatever assessment, planning, marking and feedback practices are adopted in your school, they will need regular review to ensure that they remain fit for purpose. Take a moment to reflect on this on a regular basis. Is what you are doing day to day serving you and your pupils well?

- Who can you work with to ease assessment, planning, marking and feedback pressures?

- What is unique about *your* pedagogy within your school? Does the current range of techniques that you are adopting (or are expected to adopt) acknowledge this uniqueness?

- Build up links with relevant departments in your nearest higher education institutions that research education. Not only will this help you to access the latest thinking on key issues, but it may also enable you to influence the future direction of research.

- Resist any demands to undertake assessment, planning, marking and feedback practices that place undue pressure on you with little hope of a positive return. Admittedly this is not easy, but asking pertinent questions can help: how will this improve teaching and learning? How will this ease workload? How will this support teacher wellbeing?

- As with everything that is undertaken in schools, quality must trump quantity.

SAVE IT FOR LATER...

Ross Morrison McGill's book *Mark. Plan. Teach.* (Bloomsbury Education, 2017) is an excellent resource for practical ideas about improving your effectiveness when it comes to marking, planning and teaching, while also keeping workload manageable. There are many leads to follow within it on research and ideas to transform your working practices where necessary. It would make a great text to read and discuss in a group with colleagues for the purposes of professional development.

CONTINUING PROFESSIONAL DEVELOPMENT (CPD)

Access to CPD seems to be declining at present according to what many teachers say. Budgets have been cut and when such a significant amount of time in a teacher's week is devoted to tasks associated with the day to day nature of the job, where is the time for professional conversations with colleagues? For developing links with other practitioners? For professional and personal development? Workload is a significant barrier. And ironically this may mean that the teachers who most need access to professional and personal development that could help them to streamline work and improve effectiveness do not have time to access it. It seems that such frustrations are widely felt.

When demands on your professional skills increase and you must focus on planning, preparation, gathering data and responding to change, professional learning falls to the bottom of the pile. It is no surprise that many teachers find this stressful, especially when it means that skills and knowledge are not updated when they should be.

Some strategies for ensuring that you access the CPD you need:

- Take a look at the Teacher Development Trust website for information on what constitutes effective CPD. You will find evidence and more on why great quality CPD is such a crucial dimension of the job of a teacher: **www.tdtrust. org**.

- Aim to identify development needs that may be impacting your wellbeing. What do you need support with so that your wellbeing improves?

- If you feel that you are not receiving the CPD you need in your context, talk to your line manager. If budgets are too tight, explore ways of gaining the learning you want that are cost effective – does a colleague have the knowledge you need, can you link up with colleagues from other schools via social media, or is there a book or some research that can help?

- Take a look at the *Standard for Teachers' Professional Development* via the TDT website. This sets out what effective CPD looks like for teachers. If the CPD you have access to looks different, raise the issue as soon as possible.

━━ SAVE IT FOR LATER... ━━

Unleashing Great Teaching: The Secrets to the Most Effective Teacher Development by David Weston and Bridget Clay (Routledge, 2018) is an insightful exploration into effective professional development in schools. If you can read it alongside colleagues, it could form the basis of useful discussions about moving CPD forwards in your school.

Talk for Teaching: Rethinking Professional Development in Schools by Paul Garvey (John Catt Educational, 2017) is another useful text to focus discussion in your school on CPD.

ADDRESS ISSUES OF FAIRNESS: WORKLOAD

Workload is, without a doubt, a major factor adversely affecting the wellbeing of teachers. The way in which this issue is tackled in schools varies tremendously, and it is well worth asking in your school about the current strategies to ensure that workload is as streamlined as possible.

The Schoolwell website carries many useful suggestions on tackling workload so it's well worth spending some time browsing **www.schoolwell.co.uk**. One example is a simple strategy for determining whether a task needs to be completed: Is it statutory? If so, will it improve outcomes? If not and it won't improve outcomes, ditch it. If it is statutory, are you currently performing the task in the most effective way?

If not, change it. If you are, keep it. Simple, but effective. We have to be ruthless, though. Every task needs to justify its position on your to-do list.

As with all advice seeking to support the reduction of workload, context is everything. Each tip needs to be adapted for your needs. With this in mind, these other sources of support for workload reduction may help:

- *Workload Toolkit* – the Department for Education Workload Toolkit, aimed at reducing workload in schools, is available to download free of charge at **www. gov.uk**. The Toolkit focuses on identifying and addressing workload issues in your school as well as evaluating the impact of these actions. There are case studies from schools and related workload resources. You may find it helpful to go through this process with your school or with your line manager. The Toolkit should at least open discussion on wellbeing in your school and encourage staff to explore context-specific solutions.

- *Reducing Teacher Workload: Planning and Resources Group report* – available at **www.gov.uk**.

- *Reducing Teacher Workload: Data Management Review Group report* – available at **www.gov.uk**.

- *Workload Challenge Research Projects, Summary Report 2018* – available at **www. gov.uk**.

- *Reducing Teacher Workload poster* – This focuses on a series of tips for marking, planning and resources and data management, complete with references to what OFSTED says about what it wants to see in schools. One for the staffroom, and even your classroom if you need the reminders! Available at **www.gov.uk**.

- *Teacher Toolkit* – this website carries an enormous amount of advice, tips and guidance for teachers seeking to address their workload. **www.teacher toolkit.co.uk**.

BEHAVIOUR

Pupils' indiscipline receives an inordinate amount of attention in some social media circles, and opinion is divided. While some are of the belief that schools are in crisis because of the uncontrolled behaviour of some children, others believe that some schools have a particular issue with behaviour but in the main behaviour is not the sole driver of stress in schools.

Much of this debate is irrelevant, however, when it comes to improving *your* wellbeing at work. What is relevant is how you experience the behaviour of *your* pupils and whether that has a negative impact on your wellbeing or not.

If you think there is room for improvement, there are several strategies you can adopt.

- Make sure you are as familiar as you can be with the relevant policy documents in your school. Behaviour policies will only work if everyone adheres to them. Consistency is everything. And that requires team work.

- Request help, sooner rather than later. Ask a trusted colleague to observe so that you can discuss possible strategies.

- Be clear about what you want to achieve with regard to the climate of your classroom. Have consistently high expectations.

- Check out the support out there in the form of books, research and websites that support pupil behaviour in schools (see *Save It for Later* below for starters).

- Remember that behaviour issues are something that many teachers overcome at some stage or other. Positive change is possible.

SAVE IT FOR LATER...

Behaviour specialist Paul Dix is the author of *When the Adults Change, Everything Changes: Seismic Shifts in School Behaviour* (Independent Thinking Press, 2017). He has extensive experience of working with schools to develop policies and practices to support behaviour. If this is a focus for you, his book and website may help (**www.pivotaleducation.com**). Paul is on Twitter: @pivotalpaul

---

WELLBEING BOARD

Wellbeing is, without doubt, an individual thing. But what works for one may also work for another. If there is a wellbeing board for staff located ideally in the staffroom (away from pupils' eyes!) you have an accessible way of sharing ideas and top tips. From books that have been particularly helpful to discount codes for local businesses, podcast suggestions to offers of help, jokes and cartoons to film suggestions, walking routes in the locality to cake club rotas, there are endless possibilities. As long as the board belongs to all staff, it has the potential to be helpful in boosting wellbeing and raising spirits. And remember to keep it looking inviting throughout the course of a term!

Some website recommendations for starters that you might want to share on a wellbeing board:

- **www.schoolwell.co.uk** – for all things related to school staff wellbeing
- **www.teachertoolkit.co.uk** – for classroom ideas, teacher training and resources

WELLBEING REMINDERS AROUND THE SCHOOL

With so many simple strategies known to have a positive impact on wellbeing, in the short-term at the very least, it is helpful to have wellbeing reminders around schools. This is certainly preferable to having reminders about school-wide improvement targets pinned to the back of the toilet doors! Consider these ideas *for starters*:

- If your staffroom has a kitchen area, create a noticeboard area where recipes and meal ideas can be shared. No need to stick to purely healthy ideas! Everyone needs a treat every now and then. Cooking can be an incredibly soothing hobby and anything that encourages people to devote time to the creation of tasty meals (rather than hastily assembled fillers) just might boost wellbeing. Talk about what you're cooking, what you're planning to cook and any ideas you'd like to share. Boost your repertoire!

- Some workplaces post hydration reminders on the back of toilet doors. Hydration charts are readily available online, showing various urine colours and what each may mean for your hydration levels. It is a simple idea, but when the school day can be so busy that some teachers don't get to finish a drink, such reminders can be incredibly useful, especially if drinking water is readily available for staff. Hydration matters.

- There are posters and postcards of the New Economics Foundation's *Five Ways to Wellbeing* (connect, be active, take notice, keep learning, give). These evidence-informed ideas, while not the only determinants of wellbeing, can be invaluable prompts for teachers. Put reminders up around the school if possible (see Chapter 9 for further information on the Five Ways).

- Make help visible around your school. Put up posters of sources of support (see Chapter 5) in staffrooms and toilets, and make sure that no teacher is unsure about where to turn in times of need, both within your school and beyond.

- If your school is seeking to limit working hours (in other words, is trying to instil the expectation that teachers do not have to stay until a certain time in the evening or arrive at a certain time in the morning), make that visible too.

- Make staffrooms a haven if possible. Many schools combine relaxation space with work space, and that can work, but they also need to be spaces that support wellbeing. With budgets being squeezed, many schools cannot afford to spend money on improving staffrooms, but if ever there is money in the pot, it is worth considering how to make the very best of the space available. What zones are required? What furniture best suits those zones? How might communication be encouraged (for example, it is thought that mimicking campfires, where staff sit in circles that lead to communication on an equal level of mutual vulnerability, is beneficial in schools)? Noticeboards? Food preparation areas?

- Boost wellbeing with indoor plants. According to the RHS, numerous scientific studies have explored whether indoor plants can make our homes and work-places better places to be. Findings indicate that they can help us with both psychological and biological health, leading to an improved mood, reduced stress levels, improved air quality, reduced blood pressure, and reduced fatigue among others, so it would be worth dotting them around the staffroom at least, if not the whole school. The RHS suggests that the following five indoor plants help to improve air quality:

  - *dracaena marginata* (Madagascar dragon tree);

  - *ficus elastic* (India rubber tree, rubber plant);

  - *hedera helix* (English ivy, common ivy);

  - *nephrolepisexaltata* (Boston fern);

  - *sansevieriatrifasciata* (mother-in-law's tongue).

You can find out more at **www.rhs.org.uk**.

FACILITY TO TRY OUT STAFF SUGGESTIONS FOR IMPROVING WELLBEING

Wellbeing for teachers can never be simply breathing exercises or a spot of yoga, but these things can *help* as part of a much wider package of strategies, which includes addressing workload. But if we never get a chance to try them out because of work pressures, we are potentially missing out. It can be incredibly useful for schools to offer tasters and opportunities to try out suggestions for improving well-being. How can staff make suggestions for improving wellbeing in your school? Some ideas that have been tried in schools are listed below, if you need help to get started. I repeat, again, that these ideas will never be enough on their own, but combined with other strategies, just might lift the spirits.

- Staffroom treats, with or without sugar, may offer a temporary lift. Free tea and coffee can be a boost too, if at all possible.

- Relaxation sessions to sample from local practitioners – for example, a particular exercise like Pilates or yoga, a meditation practice, massage taster, reflexology (thought to be useful as a method of pain relief) – see what is available in your locality.

- Visits from a mobile library, or a book swapping shelf in the staffroom – for those weeks when you know there is no hope of a few hours browsing in a bookshop.

- Paying closer attention to gratitude – thanking colleagues or offering praise where it is due can boost a person no end.

- Hold a group silent meditation. Just ten minutes in a room in the quietest part of the school can make a difference, especially if the session is opened, held and closed by someone with experience of meditation.

- Remember staff who are suffering or celebrating. Flowers for births, condolences and illnesses will be greatly valued.

INDIVIDUAL LEVEL

It is important to reiterate here that these suggestions are just that: suggestions for relatively accessible improvements or tweaks that you might wish to make in your daily life to improve your overall sense of wellbeing. What is offered here is by no means exhaustive. Rather, these are starting points for you to explore.

SELF-CARE AND SELF-AWARENESS

Your self-care basics – the toolkit you can dip into when in need of care and restoration – will necessarily be entirely individual to you. The most important factor in determining what they may be is self-awareness and self-knowledge. Know, and respect, your limits. Understand and pursue what makes you feel better.

No matter what others expect of you, do not be persuaded to overload to a point where your biological and psychological health will suffer. And you are the only

---

TRY THIS NOW...

Record, in a way that suits you (write, draw, gather relevant items in a box and so on), your strategies for self-care. This might be time to meet up with friends on a regular basis, a fortnightly massage, time to read, weekly date nights with your partner - whatever works for you. Schedule your next time for self-care now. Have something to look forward to.

person who knows where that limit rests. See yourself clearly and check in with yourself several times each day.

WRITING IT OUT...

A writing prompt to inspire you to keep a reflective journal

If you want to monitor your sense of wellbeing in order to gain greater self-awareness of how close you may be to burnout, get in the habit of keeping a reflective journal. If all you want to write is 'I'm shattered', so be it. If you can start to identify why you feel the way you feel, you will develop greater self-awareness. This may also come through reading over your journal retrospectively.

GUARDING AGAINST PERFECTIONISM

Many teachers have been there. We all want what is best for the children we teach and that often means putting time in above and beyond the call of duty. Perfectionism, over-working, work addiction – these are variations on a theme suggestive of working practices that do not serve us well and are likely, ultimately, to be harmful either to our psychological or biological health.

Only you know whether perfectionism and overwork is starting to feature in your working life. If you suspect it might be, ask yourself these questions. They are not a diagnostic tool, merely designed as food for thought:

Do you find yourself reluctant to start a task for fear of being unable to complete it to a high enough standard?	*If it needs to be done, start it anyway. Then you have something to work with and a sense of satisfaction that you've made a start.*
Do you find yourself unable to let go of a task until you have completed it to the very best of your ability?	*Give yourself a strict completion deadline and stick to it. Improvements can be made, if necessary, at a later date.*
Do you focus less on what went really well and more on what could be improved?	*Allow yourself to celebrate your success, as well as noting possible improvements for the future.*
Do you not allow yourself to pause or break until all your tasks for the day are done?	*When you are working but not teaching, consider chunking time so that you get regular breaks. Even if you switch tasks regularly, this can help.*
Do you add unrealistic expectations to your task list?	*Get real! You know how efficient you are with your time. What is realistically achievable?*
Does your commitment to perfectionism at work prevent you from focusing on other issues in your wider life?	*How balanced is your life? Have you shelved plans for leisure in favour of work? Book something that will boost your wellbeing now! Theatre or cinema trip, holiday, day out, something hobby-focused.*

Do you feel anxious that you could do better when you're not working?	*Give yourself a break. Stop focusing on work in your relaxation time.*
Do you underestimate the importance of what you could be doing when not working?	*Reconnect with what makes you feel good. Devote time to it. Your life outside work is just as important. Plan your leisure time and prioritise it so that work does not bleed into it.*

If you feel yourself tumbling down the dark well of perfectionism, stop. Ask yourself, if this was happening to your best friend or closest relative what would you say to him/her? What advice and guidance would you give? 'Good enough' is enough. Give 80% or 70% if necessary. That's still a monumental effort!

Related to a tendency towards perfectionism is 'imposter syndrome' – the feeling that you are not good enough for the role you occupy and fear of being exposed as a fraud. For some, these emotions can become paralysing, requiring intervention. If you feel this may apply to you, your GP can direct you to appropriate counselling. Education Support Partnership may be able to help, too.

INSPIRATION LEVELS

How inspired are you in your daily work? Is it all a grind; roll on the end of term, each day feeling like you are wading through treacle? Or are you keen to get going? Check in – ask yourself the question on a regular basis.

If inspiration is running low, what restores you? What shifts your inspiration levels? Some ideas:

- Spend some time with educators who inspire you. Twitter is great for this, especially if you curate your timeline carefully.

- Got a favourite book on education that reminds you of why you became a teacher? Dig it out!

- Look at the work your pupils have produced. See how far they have come as a result of your teaching.

- Remind yourself why you came into teaching and who all your efforts are for.

- Seek out colleagues who seem inspired right now. Talk, observe, hang out – remind yourself of how (and who) you are when you are inspired.

We all fluctuate in how we feel about our work. We just need to make sure we recognise that, and make decisions about work when feeling more balanced. What we must commit to, however, is making the necessary adjustments to ensure we move back towards a healthier relationship with work if at all possible.

BREATH – MINDFULNESS – MEDITATION

Apparently we breathe between 12–20 times per minute. That's approximately 17,000–30,000 times a day. Yet stress, anxiety and overwork can lead to us taking quick, shallow breaths that do not sustain our wellbeing.

Pay attention to your breathing throughout your working day. Some ideas:

- Notice how you breathe. For many of us when we are feeling stressed or pressured our breathing will be more rapid and shallow than it should be. Breathe more slowly and more deeply if you feel that you are rushed.

- Learn about breathing. The Harvard Medical School website has useful information on breathing correctly with some useful exercises to help you to shed bad habits and retrain your muscles. Find our more at **www.health. harvard.edu**.

- The British Lung Foundation states that a growing body of research suggests that singing is good for lung health. Not only can it help to improve posture and the strength of your voice, but it can help you to feel more in control of your breathing. Sing more! Sing alone, sing with others, sing in the car, sing in the shower! Find out more at **www.blf.org.uk**.

Breathing can be helped greatly through regular meditation practice. If you are new to meditation, there are many websites that offer guidance but better still, join a local group so that you can learn directly from others.

Mindfulness meditation is a practice whereby we bring our attention to the present moment. In a mindfulness meditation, when attention wanders, as it invariably will, you bring it back to the present moment. You will get the most from mindfulness if you undertake some training. You can do this online or with the help of a local group. Here are some suggestions:

- *Apps – Headspace* (**www.Headspace.com**) offers guidance on meditation that is rooted not only in its ancient history, but also in the science of today. If you are looking for an evidence-informed app on meditation, this is a great place to start.

- *Library* – If you are lucky enough to have a library nearby, it may well carry information on locally run meditation sessions. Many have portals of information on mental health in the locality and can be excellent resources. Similarly, community cafes and other such spaces will have notice boards about groups in the area supporting mental health.

- *Books – Mindfulness – Finding Peace in a Frantic World* by Mark Williams and Danny Penman (Piatkus, 2011), and *The Miracle of Mindfulness: The Classic Guide* by Thich Nhat Hanh (Rider, 2008) are useful places to start.

- *Websites* – The Mental Health Foundation (**www.mentalhealth.org. uk/a-to-z/m/mindfulness**) and the Oxford Mindfulness Centre (**www. oxfordmindfulness.org**) carry extensive information about mindfulness, as does Mind (**www.mind.org.uk**) and the NHS (**www.nhs.uk**).

Those who practice meditation often report that their breathing has improved and their overall wellbeing has increased. It is relatively easy to learn, costs nothing and can be easily incorporated into the course of your working day. As a tool in your wellbeing kit, it could be incredibly useful.

SAVE IT FOR LATER...

There is a useful article on the Psychology Today website that gathers together research demonstrating beneficial effects of meditation (for example on happiness, health, productivity and more). See **www.psychologytoday.com/gb/blog/feeling-it/201309/20-scientific-reasons-start-meditating-today**.

SAVE IT FOR LATER...

Wildmind: A Step-by-Step Guide to Meditation by Bodhipaksa (Windhorse Publications, 2003) is a useful guide to meditation for those new to it and those with some experience. Bodhipaksa is a member of the Triratna Buddhist Order.

FOOD AND DRINK

There is a wealth of advice out there on what to eat and drink to help you feel optimum levels of wellness (and this is covered in Chapter 9 too). But for the purposes of day to day wellbeing while at school, try these ideas:

- Breakfast is important. Go for wholegrains, and choose fresh or dried fruit rather than sugar for sweetness. If you have time, a healthy cooked breakfast can be great.

- If you take food into school for lunch, put a little time into planning ahead. Aim to make healthy tweaks where possible – add in some raw vegetables, increase your fruit intake, opt for wholegrains where possible, vary what you eat each day, try something new.

- If you eat food you buy at school, it may be harder to access healthy food options. You know what to do; choose wisely!

- Pay attention to what you drink throughout the day. Water is a wise choice, but if you prefer to drink other beverages too, make sure you don't overdo the caffeine or sugar. Moderation is key.

- If you want to improve your diet overall, and going vegan seems too big a leap (a growing body of evidence suggests that a plant-based diet is the healthiest option), make healthy food swaps on a daily basis rather than a sudden over-night transformation. The NHS offers these ideas:

    o swap white bread, bagels and muffins for wholegrain varieties;

    o swap cheesy, creamy sauces for tomato and vegetable based sauces;

    o choose lean cuts of meat;

    o grill or bake rather than fry;

    o choose unsalted snacks rather than salted snacks.

Check out **www.nhs.uk** for more ideas if you want to improve your diet and/or lose weight.

NATURE

Such are the benefits of spending time in nature (see Chapter 9 for further information on this) that we should aim to spend some time outside every day. Engaging with nature is a win for us and this can relatively easily become part of your daily package of wellbeing support.

Whether you run, climb, scoot, cycle or walk through the great outdoors, you will benefit from your encounter with nature. Just don't save this until the weekends. You can boost your encounters with nature on a day to day basis using these ideas:

- Consider the ways in which you could incorporate encounters with nature into your daily commute.

- Put some house plants in your classroom and some pictures of natural scenes.

- Create a nature haven out of underused space in your school.

- Develop a nature walk around your school grounds for staff and pupils alike. There may even be local conservation groups who are willing to lend their expertise and time.

- Teach outside if at all possible.

- Eat your lunch outdoors if space allows.

- Open your windows if possible. Spend a moment looking out, regardless of the view.

Naturally there are some important considerations, not least ensuring you are properly protected from the sun.

CASE STUDY...

Every day I write out three things that I'm grateful for. Just three things. It takes no time and it always leaves me feeling better, however hard my day has been. I have no doubt that this has helped me since I've been doing it. I cannot imagine *not* doing it now!

WRITING IT OUT...

A writing prompt to develop an attitude of gratitude

Think of three things that were a feature of this day that you are grateful for. Write them out. There's no need for great detail. Just a word or phrase will do. If you *want* to write in more detail, feel free. Many report that this can bring about a more beneficial outlook on life. Worth a try! You may also want to try writing out three things that helped you to feel calm, or three things that made you laugh or feel happy. This exercise is yours, adapt it to your needs.

CASE STUDY...

I am always wary when someone suggests that it's possible to find a solution for teacher wellbeing. It's such a disempowering approach. Each school is unique and each teacher is unique. Improving wellbeing depends on helping teachers to understand themselves, the way they work and where they fit in the system. Yes, structural and organisational improvements can be made, but please, let's empower teachers to take hold of their own wellbeing and find what works for them.

TRY THIS NOW...

Those who live in monasteries and convents often speak about making the *choice* to live in their community on a daily basis; each day remaking the commitment to being a monk or a nun. How often do you make the choice to be a teacher? Do you choose your teaching life right now?

SAVE IT FOR LATER...

Spark your creativity by dipping into *The Wellbeing Journal: Creative Activities to Inspire*, by Mind (ISBN 1782438009). It contains creative activities, blank pages for journaling and drawing, and colouring pages.

TAKE 5...

- First aid for your psychological health is important. Make time for it.

- There are many strategies you can adopt to make day to day life easier to cope with. These will typically fall into either the things you can do at school to boost wellbeing, and the things you can do personally to boost wellbeing.

- Improving your wellbeing on a day to day basis does not necessarily mean making broad and sweeping changes. Making relatively minor tweaks here and there can have a significant impact.

- Never underestimate the power of focusing on your wellbeing on a day to day basis. It can help you see more clearly what needs to be changed.

- Try what appeals. If it doesn't have the desired effect, try something else. There is always something we can do to improve our wellbeing in combination with necessary changes in the workplace.

7

ANXIETY

ANXIOUS PEACE
Psychiatrist SELF-CARE sleep
rest DEPRESSION ANXIETY
consumerism overwork PANIC
perfectionism GP THREAT

TEACHERS AND ANXIETY

It is near impossible to know for certain how many teachers are suffering from a clinically diagnosable and treatable form of anxiety. There are many surveys that give us a clear indication that as an occupational group, teachers are not faring well when it comes to feeling anxious, but we cannot know how many are being treated for anxiety or how many are suffering in silence. Likewise, there will be some who do not yet know that the range of symptoms they are experiencing might collectively be called 'anxiety'.

Anxiety can be a perfectly normal and healthy response to a perceived threat, preparing us to flee or fight. A teacher who experienced no anxiety at all would be unusual. What is under discussion here is 'pathological anxiety', which is more intense and more prolonged than everyday anxiety, and may also be accompanied by other symptoms of mental ill health, notably those of 'depression' (which includes thoughts of worthlessness, helplessness and hopelessness to the point, in some cases, of experiencing suicidal impulses).

There are occasionally headlines about teacher mental health that can seem sensational when removed from context. That said, there can be no denying that excessive anxiety among teachers is widespread. From the typical anxiety dreams about a return to the classroom at the beginning of a new term, to being paralysed by the fear of entering the classroom and teaching, there are too many teachers out there suffering.

ANXIETY DEFINED

Generalised anxiety disorder (GAD) can be characterised as an overarching feeling of unease. Not to be mistaken with the entirely normal natural anxiety we might feel before a major event or a test, for example. If feelings of anxiety become part of your everyday life, rather than simply associated with a particular, stressful event, then that may be a sign you are experiencing GAD.

Anxiety is also a symptom of a range of other conditions such as post-traumatic stress disorder, claustrophobia, panic disorder, a depressive disorder, or social phobia, so it is essential to seek medical help if you are feeling anxious in order that other underlying causes for your symptoms can be addressed.

CAUSES OF ANXIETY

There are many causes of anxiety, and to an extent, each person is unique when it comes to the reasons for feeling anxious and the particular potency of the circumstances that trigger anxious feelings. Anxiety is a complex matter, and it is likely that there are several factors at play when it takes hold, probably involving genetic pre-disposing factors, aberrant neural pathways as well as faulty neurotransmitter substance release, the way in which we work through emotions, the experiences we have had in life to date, not to mention the challenges that life is currently giving us.

We can organise these factors further. Mental health professionals sometimes refer to a scheme involving:

- predisposing factors: genetic, early life emotional trauma and neglect;

- precipitating factors: losses and threats;

- perpetuating factors: absence of support, prolonged or repetitive stressors;

- protective factors: these diminish or mask the degree of anxiety, for example good mental health hygiene such as regular meditation practice, and sharing problems with sympathetic friends and colleagues.

In the context of work for teachers, anxiety typically comes from the following, although this list is by no means exhaustive:

- *Workload* – Never getting to the point of feeling on top of your workload is an inevitable source of anxiety. For teachers in this position, each new task compounds the lack of control and may lead to a worsening in efficiency. When there is no respite, work is all-consuming and there is no way of working through tasks to get to a point where workload is more manageable, anxiety will be inevitable for some. This also has a knock-on impact on other aspects of life, for example maintaining good family relationships, developing new friendships and being able to balance work with other aspects of life such as hobbies, rest and relaxation.

- *Accountability expectations* – Are your pupils making good enough progress? Can you demonstrate that progress? Can they demonstrate progress? Is your pedagogy appropriate? Are you ideologically aligned to the direction of the school or of education in general? What will OFSTED think when they call? Such questions can be just the tip of the iceberg; a constant internal dialogue at times.

- *Behaviour difficulties* – Just knowing how fine the line is between a calm and purposeful classroom atmosphere, and one in which low level disruption becomes a real threat to the peace, is a powerful source of anxiety for some.

- *Feeling unsupported* – For example, when dealing with pupil indiscipline, or excessive planning and marking expectations, is another source of anxiety, as is working in a school with policies that do not sit well with you.

- *Lack of agency* – Being ill-equipped to do what needs to be done in any given moment; lacking the resources or the freedom to make choices and decisions with regard to teaching and learning.

- *Poor relationships* – Working with challenging people in difficult circumstances does nothing for our sense of equilibrium. When healthy relationships seem unattainable, anxiety can be a likely outcome.

SYMPTOMS OF ANXIETY

The symptoms of anxiety can be both biological and psychological. Some psychiatrists also think in terms of a 'spiritual' dimension, which relates to a person feeling a deep sense of concern and connectedness to others that adds to a healthy sense of meaning and purpose. This can be especially true of people who experience their journey as teachers as something of a vocation. If this no longer seems adequately fulfilling, a form of 'spiritual' or 'existential' anxiety can arise; a predicament that may only respond to a change of situation or lifestyle.

Just as the causes of anxiety vary from person to person, so too do the symptoms, which may also vary in one person over time. The NHS suggests that the following symptoms may be experienced:

- generalised restlessness;
- feeling 'on edge';
- difficulty sleeping;
- difficulty concentrating;
- dizziness;
- palpitations;
- irritability;
- a sense of dread;
- loss of appetite;
- muscle aches;
- digestive problems;
- sweating;
- shortness of breath;
- headaches;
- nausea.

Some of these are also found in depressive conditions, which often overlap with anxiety disorders.

PANIC ATTACKS

Panic attacks are a way in which your mind and body take over in response to fear. The mental health charity Mind explains that during a panic attack you may feel as though you are:

- losing control;

- going to faint;

- having a heart attack;

- going to die.

You may experience physical symptoms such as, among others:

- a racing heartbeat;

- light-headedness;

- nausea;

- sweating;

- feeling disconnected from your surroundings;

- breathing difficulties.

Panic attacks are relatively short-lived, although may not feel it while experiencing one. Most will be over within 20 minutes. There is no typical experience of a panic attack, and therefore no sure fire way of dealing with them. However, Mind recommends that you:

- *focus on your breathing* – breathe slowly in and out while counting to five;

- *stamp on the spot* – some find that this helps to control breathing;

- *focus on your senses* – taste a mint sweet or touch something soft;

- *try grounding techniques* – listen to the sounds you hear, walk barefoot, eat something, breathe slowly, touch or sniff something, colour something, write in a journal.

It is important not to ignore panic attacks. If you are experiencing them, or even if you just experience one, tell your health care provider. Consider what it is that your body needs. This is important. A panic attack is a sign that your level of anxiety is such that professional help is needed.

It is important to add here that anxiety disorders, with or without depressive symptoms, can and do get better. Often, telling an appropriate mental health professional and removing oneself from the stressful situation is enough to allow recovery in a period of weeks or months. Rest and sleep are the key. Only if symptoms are more severe and/or prolonged will a combination of medication and psychological therapy be required.

WHEN TO SEEK HELP

It is not uncommon for people to come to a gradual realisation that the collection of symptoms they feel may constitute a clinical disorder called 'anxiety'. Once this happens it can feel overwhelming and as though you no longer have control of your responses to life's events, however small. Naturally, this serves to add to the anxiety felt, and knowing whether, and when, to seek help can seem impossible to determine.

If any of this applies to you, make sure you see your primary health care provider (for example, GP) as soon as you possibly can, especially if your anxiety is causing you distress and having an impact on your day to day life. Your GP will need to assess the extent to which you are struggling and whether you need to be referred to a mental health worker. If you have concerns about making yourself understood, these suggestions may help:

- When you make a GP appointment, ask if it is possible to have a double appointment so that you have time to talk.

- If you would rather take a friend or family member with you, ask them in plenty of time if they can accompany you, and talk in advance about what you want to tell your doctor.

- If you think you may forget some key points, write down all your symptoms and the ways in which they are negatively impacting your life.

- During the appointment aim to get to the point as quickly as possible so that your doctor has time to focus on next steps for you. It is tempting to skirt around the real issues concerning you. Don't do that!

- Remember that your effective treatment from this point is dependent on a partnership between you and any health care providers you consult. Work together for a positive outcome.

- Make sure that you know precisely what the next steps are to be when you leave your doctor's surgery. It may be that you need some time off from your teaching responsibilities, and perhaps – for a few days only, so you don't become reliant on them – some medication to help improve your pattern of sleep. Any further medication for anxiety should ideally be under the guidance of a consultant psychiatrist.

- If you are waiting for a referral, find out approximately how long this will take and who you should call if you need to chase it up. In many cases people will be assessed first by a psychiatric nurse before they see a psychiatrist. Waiting times are variable.

- If you are ever feeling suicidal, getting help quickly is particularly important, as is involving supportive friends and family members. A trip to A&E should not be ruled out.

ASKING FOR HELP

It is all very well being told you should seek help when feeling anxious or over-whelmed, but sometimes that very act can seem impossible. Knowing that things are not right for you is one thing. Taking the steps required to ensure you get the support you need is another matter entirely. These strategies may help:

- Ask someone else (friend, partner, colleague) to make appointments with relevant health care providers for you.

- If you feel you may not attend an appointment alone, ask someone to go with you, or to call you on the day to make sure you go.

- If you feel particularly vulnerable, ask someone you trust to check up on you.

- Call a helpline, anonymously if that is preferable. The Samaritans (116 123) and Teacher Support Helpline (08000 562 561) are available 24 hours a day, 7 days a week.

- If someone helps you, practically or through a kind gesture, tell them how much that meant to you. In general people like to help out and to be told that their help was appreciated is positive. Helping someone else to feel good will also help you feel good.

Similarly, if you become aware of a colleague who is struggling, consider doing the following:

- ask if you can do anything practical to help;

- offer to cook them a meal;

- offer to accompany them to any appointments they need to go to;

- tell them about helplines that may offer support (for example the Teacher Support Helpline: 08000 562 561);

- encourage them to take some exercise outside – offer to go on a walk in nature with them, or even just round the block at lunchtime;

- ask how they are doing – in person, by text, make a call, catch up on social media;

- show that they are not alone.

TREATMENTS FOR ANXIETY

There are several paths ahead once anxiety has been diagnosed. Your GP may feel that a psychological therapy is the best strategy for you (for example, cognitive behavioural therapy – CBT) or medication such as an antidepressant or antianxiety drug.

At times when we are seeking out help, especially for symptoms that affect us emotionally as well as physically, it can be tempting to want someone else to make the decisions and tell us what to do to feel better. That is perfectly understandable, but not necessarily the best path to health unless in extreme circumstances. On the other hand, some people may be in denial about their condition – or overwhelmed by helplessness – so it is sometimes necessary for them to agree to follow recommendations from professionals. It is essential to talk to your GP, as well as trusted family members and friends if that would help, to assist you in determining your next steps. The more involved you are, the better.

As well as any treatments that may be prescribed by your GP or a psychiatrist in agreement with you, there are other approaches that may help. For example:

- taking regular exercise;
- paying attention to your diet – increasing your intake of non-processed food such as fruits and vegetables;
- stopping smoking, or cutting down;
- reducing stimulants such as alcohol and caffeine;
- joining self-help groups;
- taking up a craft or practical hobby.

It is essential to remember that it was most likely a combination of factors that led to you feeling anxiety that affects your day to day life, therefore it is likely to be a combination of approaches that will lead you back towards equilibrium.

COPING STRATEGIES AT SCHOOL

If anxiety is affecting your life, there are some strategies you can employ at work to help to minimise its negative impact. Try these as food for thought:

- *Analyse* – Aim to identify precisely what it is about your work that is causing you anxiety at this time (not historically, not in the future, but right here and now). If it is workload, be specific about what element is the culprit. The more precise you can be the better, as solutions can be more finely targeted.

- *Communicate* – Talk to a trusted colleague about how you are feeling. Be specific about why you are feeling anxious. Ask if you can talk through some possible solutions with them.

- *Avoid mood-hoovers* – Stay away, as far as possible, from those who add to your anxiety. If you feel drained by a colleague or struggle with the general atmosphere in the staffroom, keep your distance where possible until you feel stronger. Self-care is essential here.

- *Find your outlet* – Something will help you to feel better *now*, so aim to identify what that is. That is not to diminish *in any way* the need for professional care when you are experiencing anxiety, but it is a nudge to give yourself permission to do the thing that takes the edge off the worst of your feelings. If that means demoting work in your list of priorities, so be it. What is your outlet? A walk? Favourite music? Getting lost in a book? Cooking a meal? Meeting a friend? Singing? Whatever it is, do it now.

- *Create your haven* – Schools are not typically known for their beautifully designed spaces for teachers to have some downtime. But is there *anywhere* in the building or outside that you can retreat to for some calm? Or better still, can you suggest a space that can be cultivated as a calm retreat for staff?

Whatever approach you take to coping with anxiety at school, be sure to see these strategies in the context of a wider approach that is preferably supported by your health care provider. There is no shame whatsoever in seeking support.

Many people find safety and security, together with caring people they know they can trust, in the context of a faith group or tradition. There is good evidence that people who acknowledge the 'spiritual' aspects of their lives suffer less frequently from anxiety and depression and their episodes tend to be shorter and milder too.

SAVE IT FOR LATER...

There are many sources of help and advice for anxiety. The internet is a good place to start, but aim for authoritative sites such as:

- **www.anxietyuk.org.uk**
- **www.turn2me.org**

(Continued)

(Continued)

- **www.mind.org.uk/anxiety**

- **www.nhs.uk**

- **www.educationsupportpartnership.org.uk**

For advice on spirituality and mental health, the Royal College of Psychiatrists has a downloadable leaflet at: **www.rcpsych.ac.uk/healthadvice/treatmentsandwellbeing/spirituality.aspx.**

The College has also published a book, *The Mind: A User's Guide* by Raj Persaud (RCPsych Publications, 2007).

Many mental health organisations have helplines you can call, and there is always the Education Support Partnership 24/7 free helpline: 08000 562 561.

You may have access to counselling via any private health care insurance you may have. It would be worth checking any policies you have.

There is some insightful reading available free of charge online that explores the links between modern life and anxiety levels. Try these two for starters:

- The Life Squared publication,*The Problem with Consumerism,*is available to download free of charge here: **www.lifesquared.org.uk/content/problem-consumerism.**

- The *Book of Life* chapter on anxiety is available to read here: **www.thebookoflife.org/why-you-are-anxious-all-the-time.**

Swirl is a paid for 20-page booklet offering wisdom on anxiety and overthinking. Find out more here: **https://swirlzine.com.**

TRY THIS NOW...

An attitude of gratitude – think about (or write out) three things you are grateful for right now.

WRITING IT OUT...

This is a prompt that can help you to focus on the present moment.

There are several variations of this exercise, so feel free to adapt it for your needs. The aim here is to bring your attention to the present moment, using all your senses. From where you are sitting, write down what you can see, hear, taste, smell and touch. Be as brief or as detailed as feels right.

CASE STUDY...

I came to realise, after years of health anxiety, that I was focusing my grief on different parts of my body. I'd worry I was about to have a heart attack. Then that worry would subside and I'd be convinced I was developing cancer. It was like a ball of anxiety that kept rolling around. Once I got that clarity, I could get help. Counselling has been amazing.

TAKE 5...

- Be mindful of any anxiety you are feeling.

- Anxiety typically throws up physical and mental/emotional symptoms.

- Seek medical advice if anxiety is starting to affect your day to day life in a negative way.

- There are many potential treatments for anxiety. It is likely that you'll need a period of rest and recuperation, and possibly also a combination of approaches to get you back to full health.

- You are not alone. There are several insightful explorations of anxiety and the impact it can have on our lives, highlighted in the *Save it for later* section.

8

TRANSFORMING SLEEP

RESTORE relaxation *quiet* PEACE SLEEP DISORDERS
SLEEP ARCHITECTURE
insomnia **dreams** sleep
CALM REST *NIGHTMARES*

THE IMPORTANCE OF QUALITY SLEEP

Good quality sleep can be our passport to a more manageable day. When we are rested we may find it easier to be relaxed and find that our tolerance for dealing with what the day has in store is at its best. When sleep is interrupted or fitful, perhaps filled with anxiety, we cannot face the day with the same enthusiasm as we might after a great night's sleep.

It's not just about our emotional wellbeing though. Lack of good quality sleep has long been thought to contribute to a worsening of physical health too. Research tells us that those with a history of poor sleep may suffer more depression, heart disease, obesity and diabetes than those who sleep peacefully each night.

Whether we are disturbed by others while we sleep (for example, through snoring, noise or light pollution), we struggle to fall asleep, we can get to sleep but can't stay asleep, or we simply wake feeling groggy and tired, we owe it to ourselves to find ways of improving our sleep so that we can feel properly restored each morning.

THE LOWDOWN ON SLEEP

It's a much quoted statistic that we spend a third of our lives in bed, even if we're not actually sleeping! But it's probably likely that many of us are not familiar with what great sleep looks and feels like and how we might best achieve it.

While theories abound about why we sleep, we're not entirely certain of its purpose. But it is thought to play an important part in immunity, metabolism and learning, among other things.

According to sleep experts, we should aim to get at least seven hours of sleep each night (four cycles – see below), but it's fair to say that a good proportion of teachers don't manage that, for a range of reasons. Most who suffer from poor sleep will know the impact of another broken night on mood, motivation, perception, judgement and efficiency. But poor sleep may also mean we have less willpower (making unwise food choices at break time, perhaps) and a weakened immune system, making us vulnerable to every bug doing the rounds. Sounds familiar? As highlighted by Harvard Medical School's Healthy Sleep website (see below), sleep is one of the three pillars of health, alongside nutrition and exercise. If we ignore sleep quality in its various stages, we will most likely suffer consequences.

HEALTHY SLEEP PATTERNS: SLEEP ARCHITECTURE

Healthy sleep ideally involves five or six cycles of about 90 minutes each consisting of:

- drowsiness and light sleep, going deeper into;
- deep sleep (non-rapid eye movement);
- rapid eye movement (REM) sleep (associated with dreaming).

There is more deep sleep in the earlier part of the night and more REM sleep towards morning. It is thought that deep sleep could be associated with the body's physical recovery from exertion, whereas REM sleep could be more connected to psychological recovery and maintaining well-being. It may also have a role in consolidating memories.

Sleep architecture can be disturbed by alcohol and drug use (whether prescribed or otherwise), so that sleep can be less restful than it might be.

The term 'insomnia' simply means having difficulty sleeping. There are several types of insomnia. Having difficulty falling asleep may be associated with anxiety, whereas falling asleep quickly but having difficulty staying asleep may be associated with depression. To complicate things further, both types may occur at the same time. It really is advisable to seek medical advice if you think that you may be struggling with insomnia.

When insomnia leads to extreme sleep deprivation, this can lead to gross disorientation and hallucinations.

TACKLING SLEEP DISORDERS

There are medical conditions and psychological disorders that can have a direct impact on the quality of the sleep that you experience. For example, movement disorders, narcolepsy, breathing disorders and urinary frequency all impact how well you sleep. Similarly, some medications can disrupt sleep. It is vitally important that you discuss any concerns you have about your sleeping habits and symptoms with your primary health care practitioner (usually this would be your GP). Don't struggle on alone or resort to self-medication/treatment. Seek help sooner rather than later so that you can be diagnosed and treated appropriately.

Night sedation, which is medication prescribed to assist people sleeping, works by inducing drowsiness so that sleep comes more easily. However, it can also distort sleep architecture, leading to an unnatural pattern of sleep, so it is best taken for short periods only, or, if appropriate, intermittently. If taking medication to support sleep, brief (2–4 nights) or infrequent use (once every second or third night) is thought to be the best way to help restore normal sleep *and* to reduce the very real risk of becoming dependent (addicted) and tolerant (needing higher doses over time to achieve the same effect).

PRACTICAL IDEAS FOR IMPROVING SLEEP

The following section is provided as food for thought and is offered on the assumption that any health concerns you have regarding your sleep quality are discussed fully with your GP.

There's no prize for being sleep deprived; no 'hero' status for clocking up just a few hours of rest. In fact, lack of sleep is actually dangerous, leading to poor judgement and accidents. The key question is what's the key to transforming sleep for teachers whose workload may dictate a day long on work and short on rest and relaxation?

Naturally, there are no easy answers. And understandably, the best route to improved sleep is the one we work out for ourselves that suits our needs best.

That said, there are some general ideas that are thought to support improved sleep that may help you on your journey to better rest. Remember, seek professional help if sleep is an issue for you. These ideas may also support you:

- *Know your needs* – If you don't know how long your body needs to sleep each night, aim to find out. Too little and we all know how cranky and unsettled we can feel. Too much, though, can lead to sluggishness and headaches. What's your optimum sleep length? Research suggests that this should be at least seven hours. Eight hours is great for some while others need nine or ten hours. Finding out what works best for you can be difficult, especially if you are used to functioning on too little sleep, but a sleep diary may help you to observe subtle differences in the way you feel.

- *Move more* – Build some exercise into each day. This doesn't necessarily mean a trip to a gym. Just being more active works. More steps, during your working day, to and from work or during the evening can be enough to induce better quality sleep. Walk a little more and a little faster whenever you can.

- *Develop healthy habits* – Get into sound sleeping habits that don't alter significantly through the week and weekend. Aim to go to bed at roughly the same time each night and maintain that habit even through holidays and time spent away. Occasional deviations are not going to harm you, but good habits just might help. There is some evidence that catching up on sleep by having a lie-in at the weekend can be restorative. It is no substitute, though, for getting five or six cycles (7.5–9 hours) on a regular nightly basis.

- *Go easy on caffeine* – Check your caffeine intake. Coffee is the obvious culprit, but there is also caffeine in tea, chocolate, some pain killers, some energy drinks and some soft drinks. Do an audit of your daily intake of food and drink to assess roughly how much caffeine you are consuming. Aim to cut down, at least after noon. Other substances may interfere with good quality sleep too, for example nicotine and alcohol (see above).

- *Limit technology and other forms of mental stimulation before bed* – Switch off your phone and computer – there are many reasons why giving yourself a break from your gadgets from evening until morning is a good idea. There are real concerns about the effect of screen light on our ability to relax enough to fall asleep. In addition, what we are reading or looking at may also be stressing us rather than inducing great sleep. Scrolling though social media may offer a little bit of entertainment and perhaps even some continuing professional development, but we'll miss very little and potentially gain a great deal if we choose not to partake before bed for the sake of encouraging great sleep. It's also worth avoiding watching adventure movies or horror films, or anything that will hold you in suspense just before you sleep. There are better times of the day for that!

- *Create a haven for sleep* – Regardless of your living arrangements, aim for your sleep space to be as calm and uncluttered as possible. This is not always possible, especially when living in cramped conditions or having to devote part of your bedroom to workspace. But at the very least, think about soothing lighting, blackout curtains, ventilation, the room temperature (aim for around 15–22 degrees Celsius – relatively cool), the quality of your mattress, pillows and duvet or blankets, and other aspects of comfort personal to you.

- *Minimise disturbances* – Being woken up by children or pets may be a feature of your nights, but consider whether these disturbances can be minimised. It is worth considering these questions: Can pets be kept out of bedrooms? Can ground rules about the circumstances in which you can be woken up be established with children? Can everyone's phones be switched off?

- *Give yourself time to unwind* – While crashing into bed exhausted might be familiar to many, it is wise to give yourself some time to relax and unwind before going to sleep. This may speed up the time it takes to fall asleep and may even help you stay asleep for longer. Don't force yourself to sleep when you're not tired. It is better to read a novel or listen to a calm podcast or music until you're tired enough to drop off. You may also find it is best to avoid exercise just before bedtime; save that for earlier in the day.

- *Pace fluids wisely* – The aim is to drink sufficiently so that you don't wake with a headache from dehydration but not so much close to bedtime that you wake unduly for a bathroom visit. Teachers often find they have little time for proper hydration during a full teaching day but it's really important not to play catch up in the evenings. Drink evenly through the day and you'll minimise the need for disturbed nights.

- *Lighten up* – Don't give yourself a hard time about not sleeping. It won't help! If you're lying in bed awake, looking at the clock and calculating how much time you have left to get some sleep (we have all been there!), it will only add to your stress. Get up, stretch, read a (non-work-related) book and try again later on. You can normally rely on the body to re-enter its 90-minute sleep cycle in its own time. Studies have shown that people almost always under-estimate how much sleep they have had during the night. It may feel as though you have been awake all the time, but it is unlikely, although you may have been having vivid, life-like dreams.

- *Keep the faith* – Your sleep may be suffering right now, but the chances are it won't always be. Try some strategies for improvement and seek professional help if necessary. You will sleep better again!

WRITING IT OUT...

A writing prompt to help you keep a dream diary

It can be interesting and sometimes helpful to keep a dream diary, especially if your nights can be disturbed by vivid and intricate dreams! Keep a notepad and pencil by your bed and write out what you remember on waking. Do you see patterns emerging? Are your dreams more prevalent at certain times? What feeling does each dream leave you with?

If you're not a dreamer, or at least you don't typically recall your dreams, keep a (brief) sleep journal. How well did you sleep? What factors contributed? Are any patterns emerging? Are there any changes you can make?

CASE STUDY...

I was guilty of the usual: scrolling through social media just before bed, reading ridiculous 'debates' in education by people with massive egos who should know better. It would really wind me up and I'm sure it affected my sleep. So I stopped. And now I actually allow myself to unwind and if I read, I make sure it's a book - a real book - so I'm not using any technology at all. I don't feel like I'm missing out at all, I'm sleeping better, and I'm getting through loads of great fiction!

TRY THIS NOW...

Breathing exercises before sleep may calm the body and mind. The NHS website offers guidance on breathing: **www.nhs.uk/conditions/stress-anxiety-depression/ways-relieve-stress**. Just try breathing in through your nose and out through your mouth, slowly and calmly with no pausing. Notice how your jaw, facial muscles, neck and shoulders begin to relax.

SAVE IT FOR LATER...

There is interesting research on sleep so if you want to pursue learning more about how we end each day, take a look at the website of the Surrey Sleep Research Centre (SSRC): **www.surrey. ac.uk/surrey-sleep-research-centre**.

(Continued)

(Continued)

You may also be interested in *Improving Sleep: A Guide to a Good Night's Rest*, which is a Harvard Medical School Special Health Report: **www.health.harvard.edu/staying-healthy/improving-sleep-a-guide-to-a-good-nights-rest**.

The Harvard Medical School Division of Sleep Medicine *Guide to Healthy Sleep* can be viewed here: **www.healthysleep.med.harvard.edu/healthy**.

TAKE 5...

- There are no easy answers and quick fixes for sleep improvement, but there are many strategies that can contribute towards a better night's sleep. It's crucial to take an individual approach. What works for one may not work for another.

- Always check out any concerns about your sleeping habits with your health care provider (usually your GP). Poor sleep can be indicative of several physical and emotional conditions.

- The quality of your sleep can have an impact on every aspect of your life so it's important to take steps to improve it if necessary. Do this sooner rather than later.

- There are research-informed strategies that can help you to improve sleep.

- Social media interactions just before bedtime are rarely conducive to great quality sleep!

9

MAINTAINING BALANCE

Wellbeing Nature TALKING BALANCE

A BALANCING ACT

Without a shadow of doubt, the way in which work is distributed and managed in schools has a major bearing on the wellbeing and sense of balance experienced by teachers. The expectations we face *at* work will always impact the way we feel *about* work, and that, in turn, impacts our overall wellbeing.

The wellbeing we experience in our lives is *always* a work in progress. Let that sink in for a moment. The goal isn't to reach some mythical state in which we no longer have to consider our wellbeing. If we are alive, we need to focus on our feelings of wellness if we are to thrive. Many life events can destabilise our sense of balance, and fluctuations in our working lives can have a knock-on effect throughout our lives. Maintenance, therefore, is key. Take our eyes off the prize of a balanced life and we may find the slide into stress and anxiety is almost imperceptible, until we find ourselves having to address rising distress.

None of this is to suggest 'navel gazing' or excessive focus on the self at the expense of others. Indeed, it is increasingly accepted that helping others is an effective way of boosting one's own wellbeing. But it is *essential* to take on board that our wellbeing requires our focus, regardless of what is going on around us. It is also important to acknowledge that in focusing on wellbeing, we are in no way excusing the real and urgent need for ongoing workload reform for teachers. This involves a commitment at every level of the education hierarchy.

The suggestions here explore ways in which we can contribute to and maintain our wellbeing in the long-run. The goal is not to set ourselves such high aims of purifying our lives that we can never succeed. Rather, it's about finding some strategies that support us and adopting those as much as we can. We are never going to be able to achieve a 100% calm, serene and balanced life. (And we might question whether that is desirable.) But if we can improve where we are right now using some of these ideas, we'll be well on the path to a more manageable life. Taking the initiative in this way can only be empowering.

RAISING AWARENESS

While there are many strategies we can adopt and adapt to help to nurture balance in our lives, at the heart of all this must remain the need for transformation of working practices in schools. Keep the conversation going in your school. What needs to change and how? Does wellbeing and balance feature in your meetings? Are governors aware of their responsibilities for safeguarding teacher wellbeing? Is wellbeing *visible* in your school? Is there a forum for the discussion of wellbeing issues in your school? Does your school have school-wide strategies for improving wellbeing? Keep asking, keep talking, keep sharing and keep wellbeing at the heart of your school's activities.

FIVE WAYS TO WELLBEING: NEF

In 2008, the New Economics Foundation (NEF) was commissioned by the Government's Foresight project on Mental Capital and Wellbeing to develop evidence-based actions that would improve personal wellbeing. The report presented by NEF detailed the evidence and rationale behind each action, and drew on a vast range of psychological and economic literature. You can find out more about this on the NEF website (**neweconomics.org**). The NEF research resulted in the creation of *Five Ways to Wellbeing*. These have been widely disseminated since they were published, and are even displayed proudly in some schools. It's worth noting that although this research was done in 2008, it remains relevant and incredibly useful today. The five ways are:

- *connect* – e.g. with people around you; family, friends, colleagues, community. Build connections;

- *be active* – e.g. move more; go for a walk, cycle, play games, dance, do any physical activity that you enjoy;

- *take notice* – e.g. be curious; notice the unusual, the beautiful, savour moments, reflect on your experiences;

- *keep learning* – e.g. try something new; take a course, rediscover old interests, take on something new at work;

- *give* – e.g. do something for others; thank someone, volunteer, see a connection between you and your wider community.

SAVE IT FOR LATER...

You can find out more about the *Five Ways to Wellbeing* at the NEF website: **https://neweconom ics.org**.

You can download postcards to remind you of the five ways while at work.

TRY THIS NOW...

For each of the NEF *Five Ways to Wellbeing* (connect, be active, take notice, keep learning, give) jot down one thing you might be able to do - something achievable; nothing that adds to your stress or pressure!

What follows is derived from what teachers tell me they would like to know more about. These suggestions merely touch the surface of what we can do to improve balance in our lives, but they are great starting points for gently lifting our sense of wellbeing.

FOOD AND DRINK

This is not the place to offer dietary advice beyond the very obvious suggestion to eat more fruits and vegetables, keep properly hydrated (water is a great choice in addition to your usual drinks) and to keep everything else in moderation (assuming you are otherwise healthy). There are numerous sources of information about diets to follow (the NHS *Eat Well* pages are a good place to start), although it makes sense to discuss any such advice with your GP. All of that said, here are some suggestions for improving our sense of wellbeing when it comes to food and drink:

- *Prioritise it* – Meal planning, shopping for specific recipes and dedicating time to meal preparation, either at the weekends or on a day to day basis, helps to give all the processes around eating the importance they deserve. Be mindful about what you choose to eat and drink.

- *Make time to eat it* – Eating on the hoof is a common experience for teachers but if at all possible, give yourself the time and space to fully enjoy a meal or a snack.

- *Share it with others* – If you live in a family, aim to eat together as much as possible. If you live alone, consider inviting friends and family to share a meal. It's a great way to ensure you don't spend an evening working and can boost your wellbeing no end.

- *Try something new* – Freshen up mealtimes with some new tastes and flavours. Relatively small changes in the daily routines can have a positive impact on enjoyment in life.

- *Enjoy it* – Whatever you decide to eat and drink, enjoy it. Really relish the flavours. If you're eating something 'naughty' (not a great concept when it comes to food!) savour every moment! If you're not enjoying it, stop consuming it.

If you want to up your game when it comes to eating a little more healthily you could try an app. There are many healthy eating apps. These may be of interest:

- Harvest (free on iOS) – tells you what fruits and vegetables are in season;

- HelloFresh (free on iOS and Android) – meal kit delivery service;

- MyFitnessPal (free on iOS and Android) – calorie-counting app;

- EatingWell (free on iOS and Android) – healthy recipes to peruse.

In general, healthy eating is about eating more of the good stuff and indulging in the rest only in moderation. If you eat more calories than you need for the energy you are expending there is a likelihood you will gain weight. Keep your calorie intake in balance with energy expenditure and you will maintain your weight. Eat fewer calories than your energy expenditure and it is likely that you will lose weight. For many of us, it is that simple.

EXERCISE

If you want to improve your wellbeing, exercise should, if at all possible, form part of your strategy. It is widely accepted that exercise can help to improve both psychological and biological health. You can read more about this, and the relevant research, on the NHS website.

It goes without saying that before taking up exercise it is important to get a check-up with your GP. Discuss your exercise plans and goals and ask whether there is any support available in your locality.

NHS guidance states that to stay healthy, adults aged 19–64 should try to be active daily and do:

- at least 150 minutes of moderate aerobic activity such as cycling or brisk walking every week;

- strength exercises on two or more days a week that work all the major muscles.

Or:

- 75 minutes of vigorous aerobic activity such as running or a game of tennis every week;

- strength exercises on two or more days a week that work all the major muscles.

Or:

- a mix of moderate and vigorous aerobic activity every week;

- strength exercises on two or more days a week that work all the major muscles.

In the midst of a busy term, it is easy to feel that there is no time to add in exercise. And yet if we possibly can, we will almost certainly feel better. Aim to prioritise it. Set small goals at first if you're new to exercise for wellbeing, and try to find something you love. For some that will be playing a team sport. For others, something more solitary will be more beneficial. Some may love the atmosphere of a gym, while others will prefer to be outside in all weather. Keep trying until you find what works for you.

There is advice about taking exercise, fitness guides and a Couch to 5K running plan for beginners on the NHS website. Apps such as Runkeeper, RockMyRun and Workout Trainer can help you on your way.

SAVE IT FOR LATER...

Parkrun organises free, weekly, 5 km timed runs that are open to everyone, safe, accessible and easy for all to take part. Parkrun aims to have an event in every community that wants one, so if there isn't one near you and you would like there to be, get in touch with Parkrun and you could be instrumental in setting up a new run. Find out more at **www.parkrun.org.uk**.

YOGA

Yoga can be an important element of any focus on wellbeing. Whether you are already a skilled practitioner or an absolute beginner, there have been a number of studies showing how beneficial it can be for stress reduction, improved fitness and the management of chronic conditions.

If you are new to yoga, seek out a class with a fully qualified teacher who is going to give you one to one attention to ensure you are learning the postures correctly. Yoga isn't suitable for everyone, so if you are in any doubt, ask your GP if it would be a good thing for you to pursue.

There is useful information about taking up yoga on the Mayo Clinic website **www.mayoclinic.org** and **www.yogainternational.com**.

AVOID SITTING TOO LONG

Too much sitting is rarely a problem that teachers have to deal with. The nature of the job is such that we are rarely spending hours on end in seats. That said, it is worth keeping in mind that inactivity can cause ill health. If you are sitting down for a prolonged period, break that time up with short bursts of activity every 30 minutes. Research published in the *Lancet* in 2016 suggests that exercising at least 60 minutes a day can offset the negative effects of sitting too much (see **www.thelancet.com/pdfs/journals/lancet/PIIS0140-6736%2816%2930370-1.pdf?code=lancet-site**).

MEDITATION AND MINDFULNESS

There is an array of evidence on meditation to suggest that we should give it our time. There is, at present, less evidence supporting mindfulness, but there is an expectation that this may change as more research is completed. Meditation is thought to support us in stress management, anxiety, depression, and possibly even pain management and other biological benefits. It is probably fair to say, however, that most approach meditation with a desire to feel a greater sense of calm in their lives on a day to day basis.

Meditation is not easy to define. There are various traditions and beliefs about it, and as a practice it has an incredibly long history. In the broadest terms, meditation is a technique to achieve a calm and balanced state. Probably most associated with Buddhism, there are meditative practices in most religions including Christianity, as well as secular practices.

If you are new to mediation, it is well worth joining a group or taking some lessons so that you can learn some key techniques from an expert. Books can also be helpful (ask for recommendations in your local library or book shop). See also Chapter 6 for information about meditation and mindfulness.

━━━━━ SAVE IT FOR LATER... ━━━━━

Research has suggested that we can boost mindfulness meditation by combining it with movement. Check out the work of Professor David Conroy, who researches physical activity and sedentary behaviour at Penn State University, to find out more.

SAFEGUARDING HOLIDAYS

Time spent away from school is essential for the wellbeing of teachers. We may think we can plod on, showing up at school when the pupils are on holiday, preparing, trying to get ahead and generally eating into our downtime in some mistaken belief that the term ahead will be easier if we do that. Well that's wrong. All teachers need a complete break.

We know from research (see City, University of London, *Teacher Well-Being Research Project*, July 2017 – **www.city.ac.uk/__data/assets/pdf_file/0010/364987/ Teacher-Well-Being-Report.pdf**) that teachers need their holidays to recover from the stresses of the preceding weeks. But ruminating about work while on holiday will have a negative impact on your recovery. It is crucially important to safeguard holidays so that they are true breaks, whether you go away or not.

If you struggle to leave work alone in the holidays, and you think that this might be having a negative impact on your wellbeing, consider taking up a form of mediation to help you to focus on the present moment and your time away from work.

Research cited in City, University of London's *Teacher Well-Being Research Project* (see above) suggests that teachers who want to boost their recovery during holidays could:

- exercise on the last working day before a holiday (to increase your chances of releasing work pressures ahead of the break);

- start work at a slower pace when you return after a break;

- create memories during the break to cherish on your return to work.

For some, the transition between term time and holiday time can be an added stress. The regular routines of a term can mean we have little time to focus on what is making us anxious or unbalanced.

If you feel as though you have forgotten what to do in your spare time, or suffer the consequences of such a shift in your routine between term time and holiday time, you may need to prepare yourself to relax. Plan ahead. Make lists of places to go and people to see, meals to cook and activities to do. Book tickets and make arrangements, while also allowing time for pottering around. This may make the transition between work and holiday a little easier.

TRY THIS NOW...

What helps you to make the most of your breaks from work? Add to the list above if possible and create a resource that you can refer to as a reminder when work seems all-encompassing. Put your list somewhere you will see it in the run up to a holiday. Commit to it!

A CONNECTION WITH NATURE

Nature can make you feel good about life, and spending time in the great outdoors can be a tonic like no other. Fortunately, there is a growing body of research to back up what people have known for millennia, and it makes fascinating reading. Findings to date indicate that nature plays a vital role in health and wellbeing and may even help to prevent mental ill health. It is quite possibly one of our greatest resources in the quest for wellbeing.

Dr Miles Richardson, author of the Finding Nature blog (**www.findingnature. org.uk**), researches nature connectedness. His blog makes an interesting and important read and the archive is an excellent resource.

The probability is that you will feel a greater sense of wellbeing when you spend time in nature so it would be worth creating time in your schedule – daily or weekly – to get outside as much as you can. Some ideas:

- What is in your locality? Parks, nature reserves, downland, moorland, fens, mountains, valleys, weald and coast, rivers, lakes, streams and ponds – we don't have to travel far before we encounter places of natural beauty to revive us. Make a list of places to visit in your locality. Do some research to discover some unknown gems!

- Walking is just about the best way to encounter nature, but if that doesn't appeal, bike it, scoot or swim – whatever feels best for you.

- When out in nature, allow yourself to be awestruck. Use all your senses. Walk barefoot if possible. Sit. Meditate. What do you *notice*?

- Look for organised events if you'd rather not venture out alone. Your local library may have information.

- The Conservation Volunteers help to connect people with outdoor spaces to improve wellbeing. Take a look at information on the Green Gym at **www. tcv.org.uk/greengym** for ideas.

- If walking or cycling outside doesn't appeal, then consider volunteering for an organisation such as the RSPB, WWT, the National Trust or English Heritage. Working in nature would be equally beneficial!

- If you can't actually get outside for whatever reason, consider reading about nature. Some authors to try are:
  o Susan Fenimore Cooper
  o Henry David Thoreau
  o John Muir
  o Ralph Waldo Emerson
  o Roger Deakin
  o Robert MacFarlane
  o Phillis Wheatley
  o Peter Wohlleben
  o Janice Harrington
  o John Lewis-Stempel
  o Nan Shepherd
  o Gretel Ehrlich
  o Andrea Wulf
  o Miles Richardson.

- Do what you can to bring nature into your classroom. Plants can help to improve an indoor environment and pictures and posters of natural scenes can be helpful in creating the kind of atmosphere you want in your classroom.

SAVE IT FOR LATER...

Find out more about research into the benefits of a connection with nature from, for example, this review by Maller, Townsend, Pryor, Brown and St Leger available here: **www.academic.oup.com/heapro/article/21/1/45/646436**.

SAVE IT FOR LATER...

Dr Miles Richardson is the author of the Finding Nature blog (**www.findingnature.org.uk**). This is a great place to start if you want to delve into research into our relationship with nature and the benefits it can give us.

FOREST BATHING: SHINRIN-YOKU

The benefits of a walk in the woods are well known in Japan. Scientists there have posited that forest bathing, which involves using all your senses whilst spending time among trees, can reduce blood pressure, stress, blood sugar fluctuations, improve memory, reduce cortisol levels and may improve mental health.

At the time of writing, the Forestry Commission in the UK plans to introduce a forest bathing programme nationwide across its almost one million hectares of woodland. In the meantime, there may be forest bathing experiences near you that you can tap into. These ideas may help:

- If you don't know it already, locate your nearest forest/wood that is easily accessible and ideally free to visit.

- Plan some time in your diary for a walk in the woods – with friends or family if that would make you feel happier.

- Consider taking some exercise in a woodland location or in a local park.

- If your school locality is suitable, consider starting a forest bathing group that could meet during lunchbreaks or after school in the lighter months. The resources below will help to focus such a group.

- If you really want to experience forest bathing for more than a few hours at a time, there is a growing number of holidays available now where visitors can immerse themselves in what trees have to offer. A quick search on the internet will reveal a plethora of ideas.

- Do what you can to increase your experience of plants, trees and flowers throughout your working day and at home (allergies allowing).

SAVE IT FOR LATER...

Dr Qing Li is the author of *Shinrin-Yoku*, published by Penguin. This book explores some of the extensive research on the benefits to health of visiting forests.

There are also *Mindfulness in the Forest* pages on the Forestry Commission website: **www.forestry. gov.uk**.

SAFEGUARDING OUR SPIRITUAL LIVES

The term 'spirituality' is inherently difficult to define. For many, it triggers notions of religion and dogma, but spirituality is by no means purely the preserve of theology and faith. Secular approaches to spirituality are blossoming now and whether religious or not, safeguarding our spiritual lives can boost our sense of wellbeing.

Spirituality is about our experience of life beyond the material world. For some, spiritual wellbeing is a thread that runs through life offering meaning and purpose. It can inspire and be the source of integrity, joy and enthusiasm in our lives.

There is a clear path for safeguarding spiritual wellbeing for those of faith. Attendance at your place of worship or with a group of like-minded people exposes you to the spirituality on offer in your faith. Private study and immersion in prayer (if relevant) can also be a source of spiritual wellbeing. But for those of no faith, an appreciation of what Life Squared refers to as 'the amazing' can be an equally relevant and validating experience.

In the Life Squared booklet, *The Amazing*, it is argued that our lives are peppered with profound experiences that are life enriching. The booklet explains, *These are peak experiences; times in which we feel a profound sense of peace, pleasure, immersion in an activity, connection with the world and contentment with our place in the great scheme of things*. Such experiences matter, particularly in the modern world, because of the pleasure and meaning they can give us.

Spiritual wellbeing is worthy of our focus if we want to develop our wellbeing in the broadest possible sense.

━━ TRY THIS NOW... ━━

Spiritual wellbeing is in part about connection; with ourselves and with others as well as with nature, literature and other forms of creative expression. For those of faith, it is also about connection and experience of a greater power.

━━ SAVE IT FOR LATER... ━━

In his book, *Seeking Wisdom: A Spiritual Manifesto*, former physician and psychiatrist Larry Culliford defines 'spirituality' as *a word sometimes used to refer to human experience wherever the deeply personal meets the universal*. The book is a psychological evaluation of life today and urges us to develop a deeper appreciation of the ways in which spirituality and science intersect. *Seeking Wisdom* (2017) is published by the University of Buckingham Press.

━━ SAVE IT FOR LATER... ━━

Many monasteries run retreats for people of all faiths and none. This may involve spending a day, a weekend or a week or more as a guest of the monastery. Often these retreats involve a period of silence and offer the opportunity for reflection and discussion. Retreatants of all faiths and none often report that the experience is positive and that they intend to bring some of what they have learned on retreat back into their day to day lives. You can find out more about monastic retreats from **www.retreats.org.uk**.

READING FOR WELLBEING

The Reading Agency runs the Reading Well scheme, endorsed by health professionals and supported by public libraries. At the time of writing there are four reading lists available:

- Reading Well for mental health;
- Reading Well for dementia;
- Reading Well for young people;
- Reading Well for long term conditions.

There is a significant evidence base to support reading for health and wellbeing (you can learn more about this on the Reading Well website: **www.reading-well. org.uk**). The Reading Well for mental health booklist covers:

- cognitive behavioural therapy (CBT);

- mindfulness;

- anger;

- bereavement and loss;

- low self-esteem;

- social anxiety and shyness;

- sleep problems;

- stress;

- wellbeing;

- depression;

- anxiety and panic;

- obsession and compulsions;

- binge eating and bulimia nervosa;

- body image and body dysmorphic disorder;

- mood swings;

- depression and relationships;

- postnatal depression.

The books on the reading list are excellent places to start to learn more about specific conditions and strategies for developing a greater sense of wellbeing in your life.

Whether you dip into the Reading Well lists or not, reading is an excellent way to develop balance in your life. Choose a genre and go for it. Your local library may be an excellent source of advice and inspiration. Colleagues may be able to suggest good reads too.

You may also want to consider setting up a reading group at school, either to focus on books for wellbeing, or great books that you will enjoy reading and discussing. If the thought of doing this at school does not inspire, consider joining a book group outside school. Local cafés, bookshops, Facebook pages and libraries should be able to tell you what is going on in your area. If there is nothing suitable, think about setting one up. If you would rather not host at home, there may be a café or pub with a suitable room willing to let you use it in return for buying your refreshments there. You can find out more about setting up a book group here: **www.bbc.co.uk/radio4/features/book-club/running-a-club** and here: **www.penguin.com/read/book-clubs/create**.

FOCUSING ON A SENSE OF MEANING AND PURPOSE

This is a big theme for a small paragraph, but many thinkers on wellbeing consider that having a sense of meaning and purpose in your life can go a long way towards helping you to cope effectively with what life presents you with. The author Viktor Frankl explores this theme in his seminal work, *Man's Search for Meaning* (published by Rider, 2004).

In the absence of a clear definition of what 'a sense of meaning' actually constitutes, what does it mean to *you* in *your* life?

Thinking about whether your role in the teaching profession gives you a sense of meaning and purpose, and whether that purpose sits well with you, can be enlightening. Workload aside, there are many positives about teaching:

- helping to influence children's lives;
- passing on knowledge and skills;
- sharing a joy of learning;
- building on pedagogies from the past to improve teaching in the present;
- developing kindness in young people;
- working in a community with shared purpose and values;
- being part of the wider education profession of Early Years, Primary, Secondary, Further Education and Higher Education.

What would you add?

BEING CREATIVE

There is a growing body of evidence showing that creativity has a beneficial effect on our lives. There are many ways in which we are creative, and for some, that creativity is so enmeshed in their way of being that it is a crucial dimension of their lives.

We are all creative to a greater or lesser extent, and we all engage in creative activities, again, to a greater or lesser extent. But it may help us to boost our creativity so that we can commit to doing more for the sake of our wellbeing.

First, think about how you like to be creative. Through work? Hobbies? Through everyday tasks such as food preparation, maintaining a healthy living space, and caring for others? How can you expand the existing ways that you are at creativity? Then consider if you can you add in a dose or two of creativity to boost your enjoyment of life? Some ideas for you. Examples are by no means exhaustive!

- write – poems, stories, memoir, diary;

- draw – pencil, pen, colour, black and white, electronic;

- colour – therapeutic colouring books, abstract design;

- paint – landscapes, people, abstract;

- cook – new ingredients, new recipes;

- sing – alone, in a choir, a group, classical, rock, gospel, folk;

- dance – alone, with others, free form, ballet, ballroom, latin, traditional;

- develop knowledge – self-taught, through a class, in person, online;

- act – in a group, amateur production, play reading;

- be inspired – people who inspire you, talks, readings, theatre, music;

- visit – galleries and museums, bookshops and restaurants;

- ideas – keep a notebook, a folder of clippings, quotes that inspire;

- make – knit, sew, sculpt, crochet, junk model;

- make music – alone, with others;

- grow – food, plants, a 'sacred' space;

- play – board games, card games.

Get creative. Enjoy yourself. Allow yourself the time to be productive (or unproductive) in a way that is entirely unrelated to school work. You cannot lose, apart from, perhaps, financially if you become addicted to buying resources for your creativity!

SAVE IT FOR LATER...

If you want to explore research into creativity, the University of York has a particular focus on understanding creativity as a multi-disciplinary concept spanning many research disciplines and departments. Find out more here: **www.york.ac.uk/research/themes/creativity**.

SAVE IT FOR LATER...

Many books seek to offer insights into developing creativity. For example, Julia Cameron's *The Artist's Way: A Course in Discovering and Recovering Your Creative Self* (MacMillan, 1997) is a twelve-week-long programme of exercises and explorations to help you to nurture your creativity. Most libraries and bookshops will carry a copy.

CREATIVE WRITING

Developing a habit of writing in response to the challenges of your working life may have a beneficial impact as numerous research studies into writing for personal development show (see, for example, the work of Dr Celia Hunt, Fiona Sampson and Gillie Bolton). If you are new to reflective writing, these initial steps may help:

- Get the basics organised first – what do you want to write in or on? If writing by hand, what implement works best for you?

- Who is your reader? Who are you writing for? Will you publish?

- When is the best time for you to write? At the end of the day? In the early morning when your home is peaceful? As and when time dictates?

- Commit to writing a certain amount over the course of a week. Habits take time to establish so don't be too hard on yourself.

- Play with genres to find what suits. For example, non-fiction, fiction, poetry, essay, graphic novel and so on.

- Listen. This is a crucial element of great writing. Listen to yourself and the words you choose to speak, listen to your colleagues and the way they express themselves, listen to podcasts, the radio, and any other space in which the spoken word is predominant.

- Write. Make space. Make time.

SAVE IT FOR LATER...

If you want to find out more about the theory behind creative writing for personal development, a good place to start is *The Self on the Page: Theory and Practice of Creative Writing in Personal Development* by Celia Hunt and Fiona Sampson (Jessica Kingsley Publishers, 1998).

If you are considering running a creative writing workshop in your school as part of its CPD offering to staff members, you may find this book useful: *Writing Works: A Resource Handbook for Therapeutic Writing Workshops and Activities*, edited by Gillie Bolton, Victoria Field and Kate Thompson (Jessica Kingsley Publishers, 2006).

BEING MINDFUL OF OUR OWN NEEDS

The core message of this book is the need to develop in ourselves an understanding of what wellbeing means *to us*. It is about acknowledging that there is no single approach to wellbeing that will work for all teachers, and about equipping teachers to reflect on and speak up about their experience as a teacher.

It can help for teachers to talk about their experience of wellbeing and the pursuit of balance in their lives, but we have to keep in mind at all times that this is ultimately a path that we must tread alone. Discovering what will support us along the way is an ongoing quest and the answers at any one time will be unique to us and our circumstances. Be mindful of that and cut yourself some slack. You are doing the best you can at any given moment.

CASE STUDY...

At the start of each term I plot out my treat days. These are days when I do no work and actually plan something I really want to do, rather than let the day drift. I make sure I don't have to wait too long. These days are totally sacred for me and my family. But if I didn't plan well ahead, the time would get sucked up by school work.

TRY THIS NOW...

Ten ways to a greater sense of calm:

1. listen to your favourite piece of classical music;

2. read your favourite author for ten minutes;

3. look at some of your favourite photos;

4. call a loved one;

5. dance (like no one is watching);

6. stretch;

7. sing out loud;

8. sigh and breathe deeply;

9. sit in nature (or look at photos of nature);

10. hug someone (consenting, of course!).

SAVE IT FOR LATER...

The author Matt Haig has written extensively on wellness and tweets regularly on this theme. His books may be of interest to you: *Reasons to Stay Alive* and *Notes on a Nervous Planet* are great places to start (Canongate Books).

WRITING IT OUT...

A writing prompt to inspire you to reflect on your quest for wellbeing

Keep a journal of reflections on your working life and your quest for balance overall. Keep it simple at first. After a few weeks, review what you have written. Can you see any common themes? Are there any emerging issues that need your attention? Has the process helped you to gain clarity on a particular issue? If the process works for you, aim to write a little more if that feels right.

TAKE 5...

- Maintaining balance in your life will always be an ongoing project. We should never be complacent about wellbeing.

- Maintaining balance is always a personal journey. We may pick up tips and support from others, but ultimately we are responsible for our own path to wellbeing and for determining what works for us. And that is empowering.

- There are certain keys to maintaining balance in our lives that we should pay particular attention to. *The Five Ways to Wellbeing* are an excellent place to start, and are easily accessible prompts for maintaining wellbeing.

- It can be best to select one or two strategies for improving balance rather than overloading ourselves with change from all angles.

- There are many other evidence-informed strategies that can help us to maintain balance in our lives. What is presented here is just a starting point.

AFTERWORD

Teacher wellbeing must remain in our sights if we are to go any distance towards tackling the recruitment and retention issues that many schools are facing. But that's not all. We simply cannot continue to sacrifice teachers, week after week, month after month, year after year, for want of a manageable career that enables all to have a vibrant and rewarding life outside the classroom. Nurturing our own wellbeing is, of course, vitally important, but we must take great care not to adjust to fit a fundamentally flawed system, if that is what we have.

Since I began writing on teacher wellbeing two decades ago, there has been a marked increase in the numbers of people willing to talk openly about how they are feeling and about how work impacts their wellbeing. This can only be a good thing. We have to maintain that progress and ensure that teachers of today and tomorrow feel able to be open about their mental health. This is an important stage on the path to recovery. Without talk can there be help? Without witness to the traumas undergone by too many who have devoted their lives to teaching others, can there be commitment to change? Let there be no silence. Teacher wellbeing must rest at the very heart of what happens in education. Where wellbeing is compromised, may teachers talk, may they receive training and development on getting and staying well at work, and may school leaders take swift action on the underlying causes of stress in each school.

Our wellbeing at work must begin with a developing understanding of what wellbeing means for us as individuals. System-level change is of course welcome and essential, but if we do not simultaneously allow ourselves the opportunity to come to self-knowledge about what wellbeing actually means for us on a day to day level, changes within the institutions that we work in will only scratch the surface of what is needed.

The ideas in this book are a starting point, and I truly hope that they have supported your quest for wellbeing and balance, and triggered a plan for action that suits your needs. Perhaps they can form the basis of initial discussions in your school about teacher wellbeing. Whichever way you use these thoughts on wellbeing, I wish you well.

TAKE FIVE...

- Wellbeing for teachers rests on workload and working conditions.

- The solutions to teacher wellbeing can be teacher-led to a certain extent through excellent strategies to streamline work in schools, but they must also be policy-led. Teacher wellbeing should occupy the highest place on policymakers' agendas. After all, research tells us that if we get wellbeing right, it contributes to higher productivity at work and better health. Not placing it at the centre of our focus seems folly.

- There are evidence-informed strategies that we can utilise to boost overall wellbeing. Pursuing these to support our wellbeing in the widest sense can help us to thrive.

- There are numerous sources of support for teachers in need. The Education Support Partnership is a great place to start. No-one needs to suffer alone.

- The pursuit of wellbeing is about balance. *Your* balance. Not a balance that suits your school or your employer, but balance that works for *you*. Finding what works for you is an ongoing process.

SOME READING

There is a growing body of research on wellbeing generally, and teacher wellbeing specifically. While I would emphasise that it is of vital importance that you focus on yourself, on your needs, and on your responses to your attempts to analyse and improve your wellbeing, it can also be useful to see what research tells us more generally. Wellbeing is always personal though – never forget that!

The resources listed here are intended as a mere starting point. I hope that they may inspire you as you seek to improve your wellbeing.

SPIRITUALITY

If you are keen to explore more about spirituality and wellbeing, a good reference point would be *Handbook of Religion and Health*, second edition, by Harold G Koenig, Dana E King and Verna Benner Carson, published by Oxford University Press, 2012. This is a seminal work on spirituality, religion and health.

Larry Culliford's book, *Seeking Wisdom: A Spiritual Manifesto* (University of Buckingham Press, 2018) offers much food for thought and practical, evidence-informed advice.

Dr Tim O'Brien's *Inner Story: Understand Your Mind. Change Your World* (CreateSpace Independent Publishing Platform, 2015) is also worth exploring.

For a solid overview of spirituality, *Spirituality: A Very Short Introduction* by Philip Sheldrake (OUP, 2012) is useful.

HAPPINESS

The theme of 'happiness' has been covered in detail from a range of perspectives in self-help books for several decades now. There are some organisations that offer food for thought on the creation of a happy life. Take a look at Life Squared (**www.lifesquared.org.uk**) and Action for Happiness (**www.actionforhappiness.org**); both carry usable resources to help with the exploration of what can make us happy. You may also be interested in the School of Life (**www.schooloflife.com**) which carries advice, guidance and content to get your teeth into!

READING FOR WELLBEING

Reading Well (@readingagency) has a very useful website (**www.reading-well.org.uk**) which lists books to help mental health. There are currently four lists available – *Reading Well for Mental Health*, *Reading Well for Dementia*, *Reading Well for Young People* and *Reading Well for Long Term Conditions*. These 'Books on Prescription' have been chosen according to an evidence base supporting the value of reading to boost mental health and wellbeing.

Many libraries are promoting mental health through displays and reading groups. It would be worth finding out if there is anything like this going on in your area.

RELAXATION, STRESS MANAGEMENT AND MINDFULNESS

There are numerous podcasts, CDs and DVDs of guided meditations and relaxations. Whether you like them or not is highly personal so it is worth giving some a try to see what suits. Search on YouTube or Spotify for guided breathing or guided meditation. The Fearless Soul series is popular.

The Harvard Health Publishing pages of the Harvard Medical School (**www.health.harvard.edu**) offer useful information on health and wellbeing. Look out for specific reports on stress and keeping mind and mood healthy.

The NHS website is a useful source of information on relaxation, stress management and mindfulness: **www.nhs.uk**.

Mindfulness is explored in detail at **www.mindful.org**, and at www.bemindful.co.uk from the Mental Health Foundation.

It is well worth browsing the health and wellbeing shelves of reputable bookshops for ideas; the range is immense now and finding a text that suits is key.

WRITING FOR PERSONAL DEVELOPMENT

It has long been established that creative writing can have a role to play in boosting personal wellbeing. If you want to explore this further, consider joining

Lapidus (**www.lapidus.org.uk**). Lapidus, described as 'the words for wellbeing association', provides 'networks and information for people interested in writing and creativity for personal development and in working with others'.

Books on writing for wellbeing include:

Writing for Wellbeing by Patricia McAdoo, Columba Press, 2013

49 Ways to Write Yourself Well by Jackee Holder, Step Beach Press, 2013

Expressive Writing: Words That Heal by James W Pennebaker and John F Evans, Idyll Arbor, 2014

You may also be interested in the work of the National Association of Writers in Education (**www.nawe.co.uk**), whose mission is to 'further knowledge, understanding and enjoyment of Creative Writing and to support good practice in its teaching and learning at all levels'.

CONTINUING PROFESSIONAL AND PERSONAL DEVELOPMENT

The Teacher Development Trust is a great place to start if you are interested in finding out more about effective professional and personal development: **www.tdtrust.org**.

There may be local TeachMeets to get involved with. These will usually be advertised in local networks or via social media. The Teacher Toolkit website has advice on organising a TeachMeet if you want to start something up in your locality.

A number of BrewEd events have taken place in pubs around the country. These are informal meet-ups where teachers share expertise over a drink of choice. Take a look at @BrewEd2017 on Twitter for further information.

The teacher unions such as the National Education Union (**www.neu.org.uk**) are sources of information on professional and personal development. The Chartered College of Teaching will also be a source of valuable information on your ongoing development as well as issues related to wellbeing (**www.chartered.college**).

A browse of education accounts on Twitter will reveal a wide range of professional learning events taking place from various pedagogical or philosophical perspectives.

RETREAT

There are occasions when a temporary withdrawal from the world is the best path towards improved wellbeing. There are numerous retreats available, both secular and religious, extravagant and frugal.

The Retreat Company lists a range of retreats both in the UK and overseas. **www. theretreatcompany.com**.

The Retreat Houses of the English Benedictine Congregation are listed at **www. benedictines.org.uk/our-houses**. They offer a range of retreats for people of all religions and none.

The Society of Saint Francis offers retreats, details of which can be found on the website **www.franciscans.org.uk**.

An internet search will reveal a wide range of other retreat options including Buddhist retreats, yoga retreats, meditation and mindfulness retreats and more.

THE LIFE² LIBRARY

Listed below are a number of books on different themes that are interesting, enjoyable, challenging, important or all of these things from the organisation, Life². They add to the list from time to time so you can send suggestions for inclusion to info@lifesquared.org.uk.

ETHICAL LIVING

Hickman, Leo. *A Good Life*, Eden Project Books, London, 2005

Jones E, Haenfler R and Johnson B with Klocke B. *The Better World Handbook*, New Society Publishers, Canada, 2001

FINDING A BETTER LIFE

Csikszentmihalyi, Mihaly. *Flow: How to Achieve Happiness*, Rider, London, 2002

Docwra, Richard. *Modern Life: As Good As It Gets?*, Green Books, Dartington, 2008

Hodgkinson, Tom. *How to be Idle*, Penguin Books, London, 2005

Honoré, Carl. *In Praise of Slow*, Orion Books, London, 2005

Layard, Richard. *Happiness: Lessons from a New Science*, Penguin, London, 2006

Russell, Bertrand. *The Conquest of Happiness*, George Allen & Unwin, London, 1943

Thoreau, Henry David. *Walden and Civil Disobedience*, Penguin Classics, London, 1996

FINDING A BETTER WORLD

Aldrich, Tim (ed.). *About Time*, Greenleaf Publishing, Sheffield, 2005

Boyle, David. *Authenticity*, Harper Perennial, London, 2004

Edwards, David. *Free to be Human*, Green Books, Dartington, 2000

Hamilton, Clive. *Growth Fetish*, Pluto Press, London, 2004

Klein, Naomi. *No Logo*, Flamingo London, 2000

Porritt, Jonathon. *Capitalism As If the World Matters*, Earthscan, London, 2006

Schumacher, EF. *Small Is Beautiful*, Sphere Books, London, 1987

Wilkinson, Richard and Pickett, Kate. *The Spirit Level: Why More Equal Societies Almost Always Do Better*. Allen Lane, London, 2009

UNDERSTANDING THE WORLD

Davies, Nick. *Flat Earth News*, Vintage, London, 2008

Dawkins, Richard. *The Selfish Gene*, Oxford University Press, Oxford, 1999

Diamond, Jared. *Collapse: How Societies Choose to Fail or Survive*, Penguin, London, 2006

Goldacre, Ben. *Bad Science*, Fourth Estate, London, 2008

Klemperer, Victor. *The Diaries of Victor Klemperer*, Phoenix, London, 2003

LaFollette, Hugh (ed.). *The Blackwell Guide to Ethical Theory*, Blackwell, Oxford, 2003

Lloyd, Christopher. *What on Earth Happened?*, Bloomsbury, London, 2008

Mill, John Stuart. *Principles of Political Economy*, Oxford World's Classics, Oxford, 1998

Nozick, Robert. *Anarchy, State and Utopia*, Blackwell, Oxford, 2003

Putnam, Robert D. *Bowling Alone*, Simon & Schuster, New York, 2000

Rawls, John. *A Theory of Justice*, Oxford University Press, Oxford, 1999

Wolff, Jonathan. *An Introduction to Political Philosophy*, Oxford University Press, Oxford, 1996

The Life Squared website carries an extensive library of booklets, leaflets and articles that are free to download (see **www.lifesquared.org.uk/life-squared-publications**).

Titles include *The Inner Life, The Modern Life Survival Guide, How to be Happy, The Mind Diet, How to Live Well* and *How to Simplify Life.*

CASE STUDY...

I work in a small school, which in many ways is wonderful. But it means that tasks aren't shared around lots of people. Workload seems so daunting sometimes that you don't even have time to seek out support. So I found it really helpful when our wonderful office lady took it on herself to create a wellbeing board for us. She sourced useful websites and organisations that offer counselling. And she keeps the board up to date and adds helpful quotes and funny cartoons. It's great and she's great.

INDEX